What Moves at the Margin

Books by Toni Morrison

The Bluest Eye. New York: Holt, Rinehart, & Winston, 1970.

Sula. New York: Knopf, 1973.

Song of Solomon. New York: Knopf, 1977.

Tar Baby. New York: Knopf, 1981.

Beloved. New York: Knopf, 1987.

Jazz. New York: Knopf, 1992.

Playing in the Dark: Whiteness and the Literary Imagination.
Cambridge: Harvard University Press, 1992.

Race-ing Justice, En-gendering Power: Essays on Anita Hill, Clarence Thomas, and the Construction of Reality. New York: Pantheon Books, 1992.

Paradise. New York: Knopf, 1994.

Birth of a Nation'hood: Gaze, Script, and Spectacle in the O. J. Simpson Trial (co-edited with Claudia Brodsky Lacour). New York: Pantheon Books, 1997.

Love. New York: Knopf, 2003.

Remember: The Journey to School Integration. New York: Houghton Mifflin, 2004.

Toni Morrison

What Moves at the Margin

Selected Nonfiction

Edited and with an introduction by Carolyn C. Denard

University Press of Mississippi Jackson

PUBLICATION OF THIS BOOK IS MADE POSSIBLE IN PART

BY A GIFT FROM JANE AND WOOD HIATT

www.upress.state.ms.us

The University Press of Mississippi is a member
of the Association of American University Presses.

First printing 2008

∞

Library of Congress Cataloging-in-Publication Data

Morrison, Toni.
What moves at the margin : selected nonfiction / Toni Morrison ;
edited and with an introduction by Carolyn C. Denard.
p. cm.
Includes index.
ISBN 978-1-60473-017-3 (cloth : alk. paper)
I. Denard, Carolyn C. II. Title.
PS3563.O8749A6 2008
818'.54—dc22
                                                  2007041719

British Library Cataloging-in-Publication Data available

Page xxvii: Toni Morrison by Timothy Greenfield-Sanders

Tell us what the world has been to you in the dark places and in the light. . . . Tell us what it is to be a woman so that we may know what it is to be a man. What moves at the margin. What it is to have no home in this place. To be set adrift from the one you knew. What it is to live at the edge of a town that cannot bear your company.

—*Toni Morrison, Nobel Lecture, 1993*

Contents

POLITICS AND SOCIETY

Acknowledgments

Many individuals and institutions contributed to the completion of this volume. I am grateful for the assistance of Rosemary Cullen, Scholarly Resource Librarian at Brown University; Frankie Anderson, Reference Librarian at Wells College; and Jennifer Sandoval, my student assistant at Wells, who all provided knowledgeable and timely assistance when I was in the retrieval stage of this project. Tewodros "Teddy" Abebe, archivist at the Howard University Archives, was also very helpful in locating the full text of the "Remarks at the Howard University Convocation."

I would like to thank the Office of the Dean of the College at Brown University for assistance with securing permissions and my colleagues at Brown for their support. I am indebted also to Brown students, Sasha-Mae Eccleston '06 and Stefan Smith '09, for discussing many aspects of this project with me over the last two years. Their respect for language kept me sharp, and their youthful enthusiasm for research reminded me to enjoy the journey.

I would like to express my deepest thanks and appreciation to Seetha Srinivasan, Director of the University Press of Mississippi, for her patience, her vision, and her unwavering support of this volume. The staff at the Press has been attentive and professional with every detail of this publication.

My gratitude to all of my friends and family for their support of me personally and professionally throughout the completion of this project is immeasurable. I especially want to thank Janet Gabler-Hover, my friend and colleague for many years at Georgia State University, who gave generously of her time in reading and discussing this work with me as a scholar and teacher and who supported me at every stage of this project. My husband, Don, closely read each entry and provided an invaluable reader's perspective on the volume as a whole. I am blessed to have his love, his patience, and his always enthusiastic support of me and my work. My children, Joel and Miriam, and all that their generation needs to know provided the greatest motivation to complete this work. I thank them for their continued interest in the writings of Toni Morrison.

Finally, and most importantly, I would like to thank Toni Morrison, who trusted me with her writings and granted permission to publish them in this collection. Her work continues to teach and inspire me in countless ways, and I am honored to have had the opportunity to bring this important book to fruition.

Introduction

In her Nobel Lecture, Toni Morrison tells the story of an exchange between an old Black woman who is blind and wise and young children who have asked her to answer an age-old riddle: "Is the bird I am holding living or dead?" Believing that the children have tried to trick her—one because she is blind and two because with a loosening or a crush of their hands, they control the bird's destiny no matter how she answers the question—the old woman chastises the children sternly: "I don't know," she says. "I don't know whether the bird you are holding is dead or alive, but what I do know is that it is in your hands."

Surprisingly, the children display no remorseful submission to the old woman; they show no deference to age or affliction. Instead, the children respond provocatively. They challenge the old woman and criticize her for her dismissive admonition to them to find their own way: "Why didn't you reach out, touch us with your soft fingers, delay the sound bite, the lesson, until you knew who we were?" They are disappointed by her willful resignation to what she believes is the small authority of their hands. "We have no bird in our hands," they tell her, "living or dead. We have only you and our important question."

The children had expected a conversation, an outpouring of wisdom, a more contextualized response than the one she gives. "Is there no context for our lives?" they ask. "No song, no literature, no poem full of vitamins, no history connected to experience that you can pass along to help us start strong?" They wanted something more than her dismissal, the throw-up-both-hands-you-think-you-know-everything retort of an adult presumably affronted by children.

Their question had not been a trick, part of a clever plot to embarrass and outsmart the old woman. It had been an invitation, what Morrison calls "a gesture toward possibility," a youthful prompt for the old woman to tell them about her life and the world that they have inherited. "Think of our lives," they implore her, "and tell us of your particularized world":

> Tell us what the world has been to you in the dark places and in the light. . . . Tell us what it is to be a woman so that we may know what it is to be a man. What moves at the margin. [Tell us] what it is to have no home in this place. To be set adrift from the one you knew. What it is to live at the edge of towns that cannot bear your company.

The old woman's response to the children is also a surprise. Instead of feeling disrespected, she is heartened by the children's critique and believes it authenticates them in a way that their riddle did not. She seems to appreciate their "talking back," as it were, and concludes after the exchange that she can "trust them now" and can begin a real conversation, indicating that they both—the children and the old woman—have been on a quest to find out what is authentic about the other.

In preparing this volume, I have thought often about this story as I have read and listened to Morrison write and speak courageously in relatively little known pieces about those subjects that are important to her beyond the fiction for which she is so famously known. In the writings collected here, Morrison reveals to us precisely the kind of knowledge that the children in this story craved: the back-stories, the value narratives, the contexts of her life that have informed not only her fiction but also her cultural and political worldview. For as the children's questions make clear, it is in knowing what defines the trajectory, what causes the tensions, what steels the commitment, what "moves at the margin" of an individual's life that we come to understand more fully its meaning.

At the center of Toni Morrison's wide corpus of writings are her eight highly acclaimed novels: *The Bluest Eye, Sula, Song of Solomon, Tar Baby, Beloved, Jazz, Paradise,* and *Love.* We know Morrison by these works of fiction, published now in twenty-six languages, some in several editions, and taught and written about throughout the world. Her novels cover a grand canvas of African American life and American society. They are passionate and robust tales that are made timeless by their rich incorporation of myth, music, folklore, and history. While she is a careful wordsmith and widely praised for her deft use of language, Morrison is also forthright in her claim that she does not write to engage a private indulgence of her imagination. Hers is not art for art's sake. "I write," she says, "what I have recently be-gun to call village literature, fiction that is really for the village, for the tribe. . . . I think long and carefully about what my novels ought to do. They should clarify the roles that have become obscured; they ought to identify those things in the past that are useful and those things that are not; and they ought to give nourishment."[1] And each of her novels is an artistic creation imbued with the culture and the

---

1. "The Language Must Not Sweat: A Conversation with Toni Morrison," by Thomas LeClair, *New Republic* 184 (21 March 1981), p. 26.

life stories of real people at real times in history. It is always some narrative told to her, some value passed down, some event remembered, some person in her community, some newspaper story or artifact revealing an essential truth about the lives of Black people in this country that ignites her imagination. So when we read a Morrison novel, we know that we have encountered not just a careful and deliberate craftswoman, but also an artist who consistently has a larger project for her art than just its beauty; we know that each novel is also an artistic commentary on life and history reaching beyond the story told at the center of the text.

Surely we could say, as she has said many times, all you need to know about her and what she cares about is in the novels. But the particular gaze that Morrison brings to her fiction and her unrelenting passion to leave, it seems, no stone unturned in her interpretation of the large and the small of Black life—the defeats and the triumphs, the remembered and the forgotten, the myths and the music—suggest that there is a broader, deeper vision that the novels are written to facilitate. What, we might ask, drives Morrison to use fiction in this kind of culturally and historically expansive way? What influences have shaped the worldview that she brings to her understanding of African American life and to the role the novel plays in its interpretation? What matters to her outside the novels even as it influences what goes on inside them? What, as the children ask the old woman in the story Morrison told in her Nobel Lecture, "moves at the margin" of her fiction that informs, orders, and gives intellectual energy to her life commitments and to her role as writer? These are the questions that this collection seeks to answer.

The essays, reviews, and speeches included in this volume were written over a thirty-one-year period from 1971, when Toni Morrison was a new editor at Random House and a budding novelist, to 2002 during the height of her career as an endowed professor at Princeton and Nobel Laureate. Even in the early days, in between editing the books of other writers, writing her own novels, and raising two young children, she found time to speak out about the things she values. She has continued this generous, and no doubt compelling, act of writing outside the margin of her fiction all of her professional life. From the reviews and essays written for major publications to her moving tributes to other writers, to the commanding acceptance speeches for major literary awards, Morrison, in every case, has shown us what matters in her life in addition to her fiction.

The works collected here are divided into three sections. The first section, "Family and History," includes her writings about her family, Black women, Black history, and her own works; the second section, "Writers and Writing," her assessments of writers whose work she admires and writers whose books she reviewed, edited at Random House, or wanted to give a special affirmation with a foreword or an introduction; and the last section, "Politics and Society," essays and speeches where Morrison addresses political issues in American society and where she takes a grand view of her role as a member of a community of writers, her belief in the power of language, and her vision of the future and literature's role in it.

In "Family and History," Morrison reveals how race and gender have shaped her worldview and her artistry. Nowhere was being Black in America given more primacy than in her own family. In "A Slow Walk of Trees . . ." and in "She and Me," Morrison shares the timeless wisdom of her grandparents and that of her father and the influence they had on her ideas. The first essay was written as a reflection on the state of Black America on the two-hundredth anniversary of the country in the 4 July 1976 edition of the *New York*

Times Magazine. The differing views of her grandparents in the 1940s regarding Black progress in this country—certain but as slow as the "walk of trees" according to her grandmother; "hopeless" according to her grandfather—had resonance even in 1976 when there was still enough evidence to prove them both right. Her grandfather's cynicism, she says, was abated only by his artistry—he played the violin, and it became for him both his "solace" and his "weapon" in the face of the hopelessness he felt regarding the future of Blacks in this country. "She and Me" was one of a collection of inspiring essays edited by Marlo Thomas to benefit St. Jude Research Hospital. The contributors recount how their lives were changed by the right words said to them at the right time. For Morrison, it was her father's words in response to her complaint about the White woman for whom she did housework as a teenager. He made a clear distinction for her regarding where to put her loyalties—not with a job, or money, or clothes, or outsiders, but with family and home. His advice has stayed with her always, she says. "I have worked for all sorts of people since then, geniuses and morons, quick-witted and dull, wide-hearted and narrow . . . but from that moment on, I never considered the level of labor to be the measure of self—or placed the security of a job above the value of home."

Her essays on Black women, "What the Black Woman Thinks about Women's Lib" and "A Knowing So Deep," show her deep understanding of the sometimes contested historical relationships between Black and White women in this country and of the ways in which Black women have endured their "double jeopardy" in America and not allowed their essential spirit to be trampled. Echoing that mythical characterization of Black women often quoted from *The Bluest Eye,* Morrison reminds Black women, in her back-page letter to them for *Essence* magazine in 1985, of their strength and their beauty: Speaking as one member of a grand sisterhood of Black women, Morrison closes the letter by saying, "You did all right. You took the hands of children and danced with them. You defended men who could not defend you. You turned grandparents over on their sides to freshen sheets and white pillows. And all along the way you had the best of company—others, we others, just like you." These articles both foreshadow and mirror the Black women characters and the relationships between Black and White women that would be developed in her novels. Ondine's heroism, Margaret's failures, and Jadine's confusion in *Tar Baby* were explored by Morrison outside the novel long before its publication. *Tar Baby* became a way to give artistic form and function to a debate that Morrison had been pondering for nearly a decade.

During her time at Random House, no work that Morrison edited meant more to her than her work as in-house editor of *The Black Book*, an artifactual history of three hundred years of Black life in America. "All of the other publishing ventures I was involved in got secondary treatment because of that book. I was scared that the world would fall away before somebody put together a thing that got close to the way we really were." *The Black Book* includes newspaper clippings, playbills, photographs, dream books, patents, recipes, and other memorabilia of Black life collected by the book's editors, Middleton Harris, Morris Levitt, Robert Furman, and Ernest Smith. Morrison and the editors searched for materials in the attics of friends and family and those who simply knew about the work and wanted to contribute. It was in these materials that she found the newspaper articles that told the stories of Margaret Garner's tragic escape from Kentucky, of the Blacks who migrated to Oklahoma and found notices that said "come prepared or not at all," and a copy of the James Van Der Zee photograph of the dead woman whose boy-friend shot her at a party.

As in-house editor, she did not just place the book in the right places where it would be sure to get promoted. Morrison also pro-moted the book herself with two powerful review essays—in *Black World,* a major cultural and political and arts journal of the 1960s and '70s, and in the *New York Times Magazine.* In both essays, "The Making of *The Black Book*" and "Rediscovering Black History," Morri-son speaks to the authenticity of the book as an impressive and un-precedented collection of artifacts of the Black cultural experience. *The Black Book* remains one of the major influences on her fiction, particularly the historical trilogy that includes *Beloved, Jazz,* and *Para-dise.* To know this work and the strong cultural resonance it held for her helps us understand how she became committed to exploring the bits and pieces of history that resulted in these three novels.

Morrison hoped that *The Black Book* would change the way Af-rican Americans thought about their history in those important tran-sitional years of the early '70s, when there was a certain ambivalence about the segregated past and how Blacks should feel about it in this post-integration moment. In addition to introducing *The Black Book* in the review, Morrison expressed a general sense of regret that in the rush to move away from the past, valuable aspects of African American culture were at risk of being lost. Her protest of the NAACP's request to drape the statuettes of Black jockeys outside the Morri-son Hotel in Chicago where the organization held its convention in 1963 is a clear example: "Instead of being delighted that the profes-sion of being a jockey virtually belonged to Black men before 1900; that fourteen of the first twenty-seven Kentucky Derby races were won by Black jockeys; that Isaac Murphy, a Black jockey, was the first to win three Derbys; that Jimmy Lee won all six races at Churchill Downs in 1907—we draped the figures and hid their glory not only from white eyes but from our own eyes." Morrison's essay makes us look, again, at those artifacts from the past and rethink the tendency to submerge and forget rather than explore their merit on their own terms.

The first section also contains two of Morrison's critical essays, "Rootedness: The Ancestor as Foundation" and "The Site of Memory." These essays align her strong commitment to family and African American culture with her creative writing strategies. One of the strategies for achieving a text deeply rooted in the culture of the African American community, Morrison points out, is the inclusion of the ancestor; another is the use of memory. She addresses the cultural tropes of the ancestor and memory in the creation of what she considers a distinctively Black text. This disciplined attention to the ways in which her novels can incorporate the nuances and values of Black life is driven, no doubt, by a commitment born of her own research and experience, but it also comes from the teachings and the life example of her parents and grandparents. This ability to see value in what the world discredits, to track the patterns of the culture and the characteristics of its members that the rest of the world ignores, is a hallmark of Morrison's writings.

"Writers and Writing," the second section of this collection, reveals how much other writers and their works also matter to Morrison. As an editor at Random House for nearly twenty years, she shepherded the work of many aspiring novelists, including Gayl Jones, Toni Cade Bambara, and Henry Dumas. And she often went beyond what would have been expected of a behind-the-scenes editor. Her extraordinary commitment as an editor is evident in the personal letter she wrote to friends inviting them to attend a celebration of the posthumous publication of collections of Dumas's poetry, *Play Ebony Play Ivory,* and his short stories, *Ark of Bones,* in 1974. She followed this invitation in 1976 with a personal memo to book clubs in New York City to celebrate the publication of Dumas's novel, *Jonoah and the Green Stone.* Similarly, when Bambara died in 1995, Morrison edited (long after she left Random House) her unpublished works and wrote a warm and endearing introduction to the collection called *Deep Sightings and Rescue Missions,* published posthumously in 1999. We easily see in this introduction her fondness for Bambara, but we also see her great respect and admiration for Bambara's craft: She was, says Morrison, "a writer's writer, an editor's writer, a reader's writer. . . . I will miss her forever." This kind of commitment to the craft of writers whom she thought worthy—even when they were not alive to witness the accomplishment—shows not only Morrison's tenacity in promoting good art but also the depth of her friendships and how far she would go to promote the work she felt important.

Morrison was also willing to praise publicly the contributions of her peers whose work she admired and with whom she shared a kindred spirit. Her eulogy for James Baldwin is a moving tribute to a friend and fellow writer who, she says, "challenged [her] to work and think at the top of [her] form." The eulogy is also an insightful assessment of the gifts of "language, courage, and tenderness" that she believes Baldwin gave to all of us. Her tribute to friend and writer Reynolds Price was part of a documentary film made in honor of Price in 1994: "Reynolds, for me, has this extraordinary combination of recklessness and discipline. . . . What he sees in nature, in animals, in people is both inventive and reckless, but he reveals it with a masterful discipline of the language." Her remarks on both these men reveal the genuine spirit of fraternity that Morrison had with other writers and her willingness to speak as friend and peer on their behalf.

As an editor and a reader, Morrison has always had a keen interest in books about African American life and history. She wrote several reviews of books published by other houses, even while an editor at Random House and later as a publishing novelist. Sometimes scathingly critical, other times filled with praise, the reviews reveal much about Morrison's own expectations as a writer, how closely she reads, her deep knowledge of history, and the vigilant eye that she kept on other writers—especially when the subject of their works was Black life. Her comments on the anthology of Black women, *Portraits in Fact and Fiction*, edited by Mel Watkins and Jay David; *Labor of Love, Labor of Sorrow* by Jacqueline Jones; and *Corregidora* by Gayl Jones reiterate Morrison's interest in Black women— both as subjects and as authors. Her assessments of Albert Murray's *Train Whistle Guitar* and Guinean writer Camara Laye's *The Radiance of the King* reflect her interest in addressing the misconceptions about Africa, fostered by ignorance on the one hand and intentional misrepresentation on the other. In an especially perceptive analysis of *The Radiance of the King*, Morrison outlines years of the misrepresentations of Africa in many canonical texts by White writers and praises Laye for countering every one of them.

The forewords and introductions that she wrote to books that she cared about demonstrated not only her wide range of reading interests but also her willingness to provide an important affirmation for the work of these authors. There are the short forewords she wrote for *The Harlem Book of the Dead*, a collection of Van Der Zee's photographs edited by Camille Billops, and *Writing Red*, an anthology of women's writings of the 1930s, edited by Paula Rabinowitz and

Charlotte Nekola. There are also the longer introductions like "The Fisherwoman" (published also as "Strangers" in the *New Yorker*), which introduces Robert Bergman's stunning collection of photos of the faces of ordinary people, titled *A Kind of Rapture*. In her introduction to Bergman's collection, Morrison gives an account of an intriguing conversation that she had with an old woman fishing in the water of her neighbor's property. After their brief encounter, Morrison never sees the old woman again and no one can account for her presence. She is left with only the fleeting memory of the woman—and sometimes doubts that it ever happened. The story provides the perfect entrée into how we should "read" Bergman's volume: "It took some time for me to understand my unreasonable claims on that fisherwoman. To understand that I was longing for and missing some aspect of myself, and that there are no strangers. There are only versions of ourselves, many of which we have not embraced, most of which we wish to protect ourselves from." Bergman's work is compelling because it offers a similar engagement with faces of people that we will never see again, and it echoes Morrison's shared interest in seeing the distinctive value of those unnoticed in society—the kind of people that Morrison shapes into memorable characters in her novels.

The final section, "Politics and Society," collects essays and speeches where Morrison responds to contemporary issues. Her commentaries on three events that have become mainstays of the media—immigration, the Clinton presidency, and the attacks of September 11—show Morrison deeply engaged in the political debates of the day. They reveal her insightful critiques on the intersections of race and politics in this country and how we can better understand the full implications of political actions if we also understand the tropes of race and racism and their manifestations in the public square. She never shies away from the controversial with her provocative comments on immigration and the Clinton impeachment and her moving meditation on the victims of events of September 11.

In her speeches, Morrison reveals her wider scope as an artist, as a champion of the power of literature and language, and as an intellectual concerned about the future. In "For a Heroic Writers Movement," Morrison calls on three thousand attendees at the Writers Congress in 1981 to shun individualism and isolation and bond together as a workers' collective in control of their profession. In this spirited and compelling address to her fellow writers, we see Morrison as more than an individual artist honing her craft, but also as a comrade leading the charge for an army of writers: "If just one resolution comes from this Congress, let it be that we remain at the barricades where we belong. We must be more than central. We must be sovereign."

In "Remarks Given at the Howard University Charter Day Convocation," delivered in March 1995, Morrison shares what Howard bestowed upon her and how, given their history, Howard alumni must be the sentinels on watch in the insidious war declared on people of color. What she learned there academically and politically she takes with her beyond the margins of her work and, no doubt, in ways not totally imperceptible, into her fiction. Echoing the lesson of the story she told in her Nobel Speech, she encourages her audience at Howard to tell the children what they need to know: "It's important to know that nothing, nothing . . . nothing is more important than our children. And if our children don't think they are important to us, if they don't think they are important to themselves, if they don't think they are important to the world, it's because we have not told them. We have not told them that they are our immortality. We have not told them that they are responsible for producing and leading generations after them. We have not told them the things Howard University told me."

The 1996 Jefferson Lecture in the Humanities, "The Future of Time: Literature and Diminished Expectations," offers an expansive view of history in the late twentieth century and how we must prepare for the twenty-first. It is a rare glimpse into Morrison's ideas about the future and the kinship she feels with other writers who have talked about time and its meaning. As we think about the future, she concludes "we should heed the meditations of literature," and instead of being stymied by a lack of vision, that we should embrace William Gass's vision put forth in *The Tunnel* and realize that "there are worlds of Edens inside of us." As she does in the Jefferson Lecture, Morrison uses her other major lectures to argue for the power of literature and language to transform us individually and to help us construct a better world. In "The Dancing Mind," a speech given on the acceptance of the National Book Foundation Medal in 1996, she focuses on the enabling power of language gained in the act of reading. Whether it is the "entitled" or the "dispossessed," reading makes it possible, she says, "to experience one's own mind dancing with another's." We see Morrison in these lectures not just as a novelist who is the beneficiary of people reading her work, but also as a champion of language generally and one willing to use her position in the academy and in the arts to argue its importance.

In "How Can Values Be Taught in the University," a speech delivered at the Center for Human Values at Princeton University in 2000, Morrison assumes her reflective role as a college professor and member of the university community. She ponders how and whether, in a postmodern world, values can be taught in a university. Despite its history, the university, she insists, must not confuse values with "religiosity" or dogma. The best way to continue its value-laden legacy is for the university community to demonstrate values by example: "We teach values by having them." This is an issue, she believes, that the university must take seriously, for if it does not, "then some other regime or ménage of regimes will do it for us, in spite of us, and without us."

This volume concludes with Morrison's Nobel Lecture, the speech that provides the central metaphor for this collection and one that also provides an important statement about Morrison's work and her vision for the kind of world that language can enable. "The vitality of language," she argues, "lies in its ability to limn the actual, imagined, and possible lives of its speakers, readers, writers. . . . It arcs toward the place where meaning may lie." This lecture remains a tour de force in its philosophical meditation on and its practical demonstration of the generative power of language.

Morrison's honest assessments and reflections collected in this volume show us the broad range of values, interests, responsibilities, and expectations that she brings to the artistic enterprise of writing novels. When we read her novels, she is the narrator with no name and the silent artist through whom only the characters speak. In the works collected here, we hear Morrison speaking courageously, provocatively, and prophetically in her own voice. These writings allow us to see Morrison as a committed granddaughter and daughter, as a woman who is part of a sisterhood of Black women, as a descendant of an enslaved people, as an uncompromising editor, as a member of a profession of writers, as friend, alum, scholar, and as an individual member of the world community having to contemplate her responsibility to the future. Getting to see *this* Toni Morrison, the one not taking us (as we are so accustomed) across a threshold into the breathtaking space of her fiction, is a very special moment. *What Moves at the Margin* opens another door for us, takes us away from the center of her fiction to the margins outside. It will engage, in-form, surprise, and provoke; and it will also reveal the calculus that describes Morrison's thinking. For what moves at the margin of Toni Morrison's impressive body of fiction are the forces that shape her both as woman and as artist: truth, outrage, hope, and love.

Family and History

A Slow Walk of Trees
(as Grandmother Would Say),
Hopeless (as Grandfather Would Say)

New York Times Magazine (4 July 1976): 104+. Reprinted by permission of International Creative Management, Inc. Copyright © 1976 by Toni Morrison.

> We are content to abide where we are. We do not believe that things
> will always continue the same. The time must come when the Dec-
> laration of Independence will be felt in the heart, as well as uttered
> in the mouth. . . . This is our home, and this is our country.—An
> "Address to the citizens of New York," by a black group in 1831

His name was John Solomon Willis, and when at age five he heard
from the old folks that "the Emancipation Proclamation was coming," he crawled under the bed. It was his earliest recollection of what
was to be his habitual response to the promises of white people: horror and an instinctive yearning for safety. He was my grandfather,
a musician who managed to hold on to his violin but not his land.
He lost all eighty-eight acres of his Indian mother's inheritance to
legal predators who built their fortunes on the likes of him. He was
an unreconstructed black pessimist who, in spite of or because of
emancipation, was convinced for eighty-five years that there was no
hope whatever for black people in this *country. His rancor* was legitimate, for he, John Solomon, was not only an artist but a first-rate

3

carpenter and farmer, reduced to sending home to his family money he made playing the violin because he was not able to find work. And this during the years when almost half the black male population were skilled craftsmen who lost their jobs to white ex-convicts and immigrant farmers.

His wife, however, was of a quite different frame of mind and believed that all things could be improved by faith in Jesus and an effort of the will. So it was she, Ardelia Willis, who sneaked her seven children out of the Sack window into the darkness, rather than permit the patron of their sharecropper's existence to become their executioner as well, and headed north in 1912, when 99.2 percent of all black people in the U.S. were native-born and only 60 percent of white Americans were. And it was Ardelia who told her husband that they could not stay in the Kentucky town they ended up in because the teacher didn't know long division.

They have been dead now for thirty years and more and I still don't know which of them came closer to the truth about the possibilities of life for black people in this country. One of their grandchildren is a tenured professor at Princeton. Another, who suffered from what the Peruvian poet called "anger that breaks a man into children," was picked up just as he entered his teens and emotionally lobotomized by the reformatories and mental institutions specifically designed to serve him. Neither John Solomon nor Ardelia lived long enough to despair over one or swell with pride over the other. But if they were alive today each would have selected and collected enough evidence to support the accuracy of the other's original point of view. And it would be difficult to convince either one that the other was right.

Some of the monstrous events that took place in John Solomon's America have been duplicated in alarming detail in my own America.

There was the public murder of a President in a theater in 1865 and the public murder of another President on television in 1963. The Civil War of 1861 had its encore as the civil-rights movement of 1960. The torture and mutilation of a black West Point Cadet (Cadet Johnson Whittaker) in 1880 had its rerun with the 1970s' murders of students at Jackson State College, Texas Southern, and Southern University in Baton Rouge. And in 1976 we watch for what must be the thousandth time a pitched battle between the children of slaves and the children of immigrants—only this time, it is not the New York draft riots of 1863, but the busing turmoil in Paul Revere's home town, Boston.

Hopeless, he'd said. Hopeless. For he was certain that white people of every political, religious, geographical, and economic background would band together against black people everywhere when they felt the threat of our progress. And a hundred years after he sought safety from the white man's "promise," somebody put a bullet in Martin Luther King's brain. And not long before that some excellent samples of the master race demonstrated their courage and virility by dynamiting some little black girls to death. If he were here now, my grandfather, he would shake his head, close his eyes, and pull out his violin—too polite to say, "I told you so." And his wife would pay attention to the music but not to the sadness in her husband's eyes, for she would see what she expected to see—not the occasional historical repetition, but, like the slow walk of certain species of trees from the flat-lands up into the mountains, she would see the signs or irrevocable and permanent change. She, who pulled her girls out of an inadequate school in the Cumberland Mountains, knew all along that the gentlemen from Alabama who had killed the little girls would be rounded up. And it wouldn't surprise her in the least to know that the number of black college graduates jumped

12 percent in the last three years; 47 percent in twenty years. That there are 140 black mayors in this country; fourteen black judges in the District Circuit, four in the Courts of Appeals and one on the Supreme Court. That there are seventeen blacks in Congress, one in the Senate; 276 in state legislatures—223 in state houses, 53 in state senates. That there are 112 elected black police chiefs and sheriffs, one Pulitzer Prize winner; one winner of the Prix de Rome; a dozen or so winners of the Guggenheim; four deans of predominantly white colleges. . . . Oh, *her list would go on* and on. But so would John Solomon's sweet sad music.

While my grandparents held opposite views on whether the fortunes of black people were improving, my own parents struck similarly opposed postures, but from another slant. They differed about whether the moral fiber of white people would ever improve. Quite a different argument. The old folks argued about how and if black people could improve themselves, who could be counted on to help us, who would hinder us, and so on. My parents took issue over the question of whether it was possible for white people to improve. They assumed that black people were the humans of the globe; but had serious doubts about the quality and existence of white humanity. Thus my father, distrusting every word and every gesture of every white man on earth, assumed that the white man who crept up the stairs one afternoon had come to molest his daughters and threw him down the stairs and then our tricycle after him. (I think my father was wrong, but considering what I have seen since, it may have been very healthy for me to have witnessed that as my first black-white encounter.) My mother, however, *believed* in them—their possibilities. So when the meal we got on relief was bug-ridden, she wrote a long letter to Franklin Delano Roosevelt. And when white

bill collectors came to our door, it was she who received them civ-
illy and explained in a sweet voice that we were people of honor and
that the debt would be taken care of. Her message to Roosevelt got
through—our meal improved. Her message to the bill collectors did not
always get through, and there was occasional violence when my father (self-exiled to the bedroom for fear he could not hold his temper) would hear that her reasonableness had failed. *My mother* was
always wounded by these scenes, for she thought the bill collector
knew that she loved good credit more than life and that being in
arrears on a payment horrified her probably more than it did him.
So she thought he was rude because he was white. For years she
walked to utility companies and department stores to pay bills in
person and even now she does not seem convinced that checks are
legal tender. My father loved excellence, worked hard (he held three
jobs at once for seventeen years), and was so outraged by the suggestion of personal slackness that he could explain it to himself only
in terms of racism. He was a fastidious worker who was frightened
of one thing: unemployment. I can remember now the doomsday-
cum-graveyard sound of "laid off" and how the minute school was
out he asked us, "Where you workin'?" Both my parents believed
that all succor and aid came from themselves and their neighborhood, since "they"—white people in charge and those not in charge
but in obstructionist positions—were in some way fundamentally,
genetically corrupt.

So I grew up in a basically racist household with more than a
child's share of contempt for white people. And for each white friend
I acquired who made a small crack in that contempt, there was another who repaired it. For each one who related to me as a person,
there was one who in my presence at least, became actively "white."

And like most black people of my generation, I suffer from racial vertigo that can be cured only by taking what one needs from one's ancestors. John Solomon's cynicism and his deployment of his art as both weapon and solace; Ardelia's faith in the magic that can be wrought by sheer effort of the will; my mother's open-mindedness in each new encounter and her habit of trying reasonableness first; my father's temper, his impatience, and his efforts to keep "them" (throw them) out of his life. And it is out of these learned and selected attitudes that I look at the quality of life for my people in this country now.

These widely disparate and sometimes conflicting views, I suspect, were held not only by me, but by most black people. Some I know are clearer in their positions, have not sullied their anger with optimism or dirtied their hope with despair. But most of us are plagued by a sense of being worn shell-thin by constant repression and hostility as well as the impression of being buoyed by visible testimony of tremendous strides. There *is* repetition of the grotesque in our history. And there *is* the miraculous walk of trees. The question is whether our walk is progress or merely movement. O.J. Simpson leaning on a Hertz car *is* better than the Gold Dust Twins on the back of a soap box. But is *Good Times* better than Stepin Fetchit? Has the first order of business been taken care of? Does the law of the land work for us?

Are white people who murder black people punished with at least the same dispatch that sends black teenage truants to Coxsackie? Can we relax now and discuss *The Jeffersons* instead of genocide? Or is the difference between the two only the difference between a greedy pointless white lifestyle and a messy pointless black death? Now that Mr. Poitier and Mr. Belafonte have shot up all the racists in *Buck and the Preacher,* have they all gone away? Can we really move into better neighborhoods and not be set on fire? Is there anybody who will lay me a five-dollar bet on it?

The past decade is a fairly good index of the odds at which you lay your money down.

Ten years ago in Queens, as black people like me moved into a neighborhood twenty minutes away from the Triborough Bridge. "for sale" signs shot up in front of white folks' houses like dandelions after a hot spring rain. And the black people smiled. "Goody, goody," said my neighbor. "Maybe we can push them on out to the sea. You think?"

Now I live in another neighborhood, twenty minutes away from the George Washington Bridge, and again the "for sale" signs are pushing up out of the ground. Fewer, perhaps, and for different reasons, perhaps. Still the Haitian lady and I smile at each other. "My, my," she says, "they goin' on up to the hills? Seem like they just come from there." "The woods," I say. "They like to live in the woods." She nods with infinite understanding, then shrugs. The Haitians have already arranged for one mass in the church to be said in French, already have their own newspaper, stores, community center. That's not movement. That's progress.

But the decade has other revelations. Ten years ago, young, bright, energetic blacks were sought out, pursued and hired into major corporations, major networks, and onto the staffs of newspapers and national magazines. Many survived that courtship, some even with their souls intact. Newscasters, corporate lawyers, marketing specialists, journalists, production managers, plant foremen, college deans. But many more spend a lot of time on the telephone these days, or at the typewriter preparing résumés, which they send out (mostly to friends now) with little notes attached: "Is there anything you know of?" Or they think there is a good book in the story of what happened to them, the great hoax that was played on them. They are right, of course, about the hoax, for many of them were given elegant executive jobs with the work drained out. Work minus power. Work minus decision-making. Work minus dominion. Affirmative Action Make Believe that a lot of black people *did* believe because they also believed that the white people in those nice offices were not like the ones in the general store or in the plumbers union—that they were fundamentally kind, or fair, or something. Anything but the desperate prisoners of economics they turned out to be, holding on to their dominion with a tenacity and sang-froid that can only be described as Nixonian. So the bright and the black (architects, reporters, vice-presidents in charge of public relations) walk the streets right along with that astounding 38 percent of the black teen-aged female work force that does not have and never has had a job. So the black female college graduate earns two-thirds of what a white male high-school dropout earns. So the black people who put everything into community-action programs supported by Government funds have found themselves bereft of action, bereft of funds and all but bereft of community.

This decade has been rife with disappointment in practically every place where we thought we saw permanent change: Hostos, CUNY, and the black-studies departments that erupted like minivolcanoes on campuses all over the nation; easy integrations of public-school systems; acceleration of promotion in factories and businesses. But now when we describe what has happened we cannot do it without using the verbs of upheaval and destruction: Open admission *closes;* minority-student quotas *fall* or *discontinue;* salary gaps between blacks and whites *widen;* black-studies departments *merge.* And the only growth black people can count on is in the prison population and the unemployment line. Even busing, which used to be a plain, if emotional, term at best, *has* now taken on an adjective normally reserved for rape and burglary—it is now called "forced" busing.

All of that counts, but I'm not sure that in the long haul it matters. Maybe Ardelia Willis had the best idea. One sees signs of her vision and the fruits of her prophecy in spite of the dread-lock statistics. The trees *are* walking, albeit slowly and quietly and without the fanfare of a cross-country run. It seems that at last black people have abandoned our foolish dependency on the Government to do the work that we once thought all of its citizenry would be delighted to do. Our love affair with the Federal Government is over. We misjudged the ardor of its attention. We thought its majority constituency would *prefer* having their children grow up among happy, progressive, industrious, contented black children rather than among angry, disenchanted, and dangerous ones. That the profit motive of industry alone would keep us employed and therefore spending, and that our poverty was bad for business. We thought landlords wanted us to have a share in our neighborhoods and therefore love and care for them. That city governments wanted us to control our schools and therefore preserve them.

We were wrong. And now, having been eliminated from the lists of urgent national priorities, from TV documentaries and the platitudes of editorials, black people have chosen, or been forced to seek safety from the white man's promise, but happily not under a bed. More and more, there is the return to Ardelia's ways: the exercise of the will, the recognition of obstacles as only that—obstacles, not fixed stars. Black judges are fixing appropriate rather than punitive bail for black "offenders" and letting the rest of the community of jurisprudence scream. Young black women are leaving plush Northern jobs to sit in their living rooms and teach black children, work among factory women, and spend months finding money to finance the college education of young blacks. Groups of blacks are buying huge tracts of land in the South and cutting off entirely the dependency of whole communities on grocery chains. For the first time, significant numbers of black people are returning or migrating to the South to focus on the acquisition of land, the transferal of crafts and skills, and the sharing of resources, the rebuilding of neighborhoods.

In the shambles of closing admissions, falling quotas, widening salary gaps, and merging black-studies departments, builders and healers are working quietly among us. They are not like the heroes of old, the leaders we followed blindly and upon whom we depended for everything, or the blacks who had accumulated wealth for its own sake, fame, medals, or some public acknowledgment of success. These are the people whose work is real and pointed and clear in its application to the race. Some are old and have been at work for a long time in and out of the public eye. Some are new and just finding out what their work is. But they are unmistakably the natural aristocrats of the race. The ones who refuse to imitate, to compromise, and who are indifferent to public accolade. Whose work is free or priceless. They take huge risks economically and personally. They are not always popular, even among black people, but they are the ones whose work black people respect. They are the healers. Some are nowhere near the public eye: Ben Chavis, preacher and political activist languishing now in North Carolina prisons; Robert Moses, a pioneering activist; Sterling Brown, poet and teacher; Father Al McKnight, land reformer; Rudy Lombard, urban sociologist; Lerone Bennett, historian; C. L. R. James, scholar; Alyce Gullattee, psychologist and organizer. Others are public legends: Judge Crockett, Judge Bruce Wright, Stevie Wonder, Ishmael Reed, Miles Davis, Richard

Pryor, Muhammad Ali, Fannie Lou Hamer, Eubie Blake, Angela Davis, Bill Russell. . . .

But a complete roll-call is neither fitting nor necessary. They know who they are and so do we. They clarify our past, make livable our present and are certain to shape our future. And since the future is where our immortality as a race lies, no overview of the state of black people at this time can ignore some speculation on the only ones certain to live it—the children.

They are both exhilarating and frightening, those black children, and a source of wonderment to me. Although statistics about black teen-age crime and the "failure" of the courts to gut them are regularly printed and regularly received with outrage and fear, the children I know and see, those born after 1960, do not make such great copy. They are those who have grown up with nothing to prove to white people, whose perceptions of themselves are so new, so different, so focused they appear to me to be either magnificent hybrids or throwbacks to the time when our ancestors were called "royal." They are the baby sisters of the sit-in generation, the sons of the neighborhood blockbusters, the nephews of jailed revolutionaries, and a huge number who have had college graduates in their families for three and four generations. I thought we had left them nothing to love and nothing to want to know. I thought that those who exhibited some excitement about their future had long ago looked into the eyes of their teachers and were either saddened or outraged by the death of possibility they found there. I thought that those who were interested in the past had looked into the faces of their parents and seen betrayal. I thought the state had deprived them of a land and the landlords and banks had deprived them of a turf. So how is it that, with nothing to love, nothing they need to know, landless, turfless, minus a future and a past, these black children look us dead in the eye? They seem not to know how to apologize. And even when they are wrong they do not ask for forgiveness. It is as though they are waiting for us to apologize to them, to beg their pardon, to seek their approval. What species of black is this that not only does not choose to grovel, but doesn't know how? How will they keep jobs? How will they live? Won't they be killed before they reproduce? But they are unafraid. Is it because they refuse to see the world as we did? Is it because they have rejected both land and turf to seek instead a world? Maybe they finally got the message that we had been shouting into their faces; that they *live* here, *belong* here on this planet earth and that it is *theirs*. So they watch us with the eyes of poets and carpenters and musicians and scholars and other people who know who they are because they have invented themselves and know where they are going because they have envisioned it. All of which would please Ardelia—and John Solomon, too, I think. After all, he did hold on to his violin.

She and Me

In *The Right Words at the Right Time*, edited by Marlo Thomas. New York: Simon and Schuster, 2002. 221–23. Reprinted by permission of International Creative Management, Inc. Copyright © 2002 by Toni Morrison.

The best news was the two dollars and fifty cents. Each Friday She would give me, a twelve-year-old, enough money to see sixteen movies or buy fifty Baby Ruth candy bars. And all I had to do for it was clean Her house for a few hours after school. A beautiful house, too, with plastic-covered sofa and chairs, wall-to-wall blue and white carpeting, a white enamel stove, automatic washing machine—things common in Her neighborhood, rare in mine. In the middle of the war, She had butter, sugar, steaks and seam-up-the-back hose. Around the house, Her grass was mowed and Her bushes were clipped to balls the size of balloons. Amazed and happy, I fairly skipped down sidewalks too new for hopscotch to my first job.

I wasn't very good at it. I knew how to scrub floors on my knees but not with a mop and I'd never encountered a Hoover or used an iron that was not heated by fire. So I understood Her impatience, Her nagging, Her sigh of despair. And I tried harder each day to be worth the heap of Friday coins She left on the counter by the back door. My pride in earning money that I could squander, if I chose to, was increased by the fact that half of it my mother took. That is, part of my wages was used for real things: an insurance policy payment maybe or the milkman. Pleasure, at that age, at being necessary to my parents was profound. I was not like the children in folk tales—a burdensome mouth to feed, a problem to be solved, a nuisance to be corrected. I had the status that routine chores at home did not provide—a slow smile, an approving nod from an adult. All suggestions that a place for me among them was imminent.

I got better at cleaning Her house; so good, I was given more to do, much more. I remember being asked to move a piano from one side of the room to another and once to carry bookcases upstairs. My arms and legs hurt and I wanted to complain, but other than my sister, there was no one to go to. If I refused Her I would be fired. If I told my mother she would make me quit. Either way my finances and my family standing would be lost. It was being slowly eroded anyway because She began to offer me her clothes—for a price. And impressed by these worn things that looked simply gorgeous to a little girl with two dresses for school, I eagerly bought them. Until my mother asked me if I really wanted to work for castoffs. So I learned to say "No thank you" to a faded sweater offered for half a week's pay. Still I had trouble summoning the courage to discuss or object to the increasing demands made on me.

One day alone in the kitchen with my father, I let drop a few whines about my job. I know I gave him details, examples, but while he listened intently, I saw no sympathy in his eyes. No "Oh, you poor little thing." Perhaps he understood I wanted a solution to work, not an escape from it. In any case, he put down his cup of coffee finally and said, "Listen. You don't live there. You live here. At home, with your people. Just go to work; get your money and come on home."

That is what he said. This is what I heard:

1. Whatever the work, do it well, not for the boss but for yourself.
2. You make the job; it doesn't make you.
3. Your real life is with us, your family.
4. You are not the work you do; you are the person you are.

I have worked for all sorts of people since then, geniuses and morons, quick-witted and dull, wide-hearted and narrow, and had many kinds of jobs, but from that moment on, I never considered the level of labor to be the measure of self or placed the security of a job above the value of home.

What the Black Woman
Thinks about Women's Lib

New York Times Magazine (22 August 1971): 4+. Reprinted by permission of International Creative Management, Inc. Copyright © 1971 by Toni Morrison.

They were always there. Whenever you wanted to do something simple, natural and inoffensive. Like drink some water, sit down, go to the bathroom or buy a bus ticket to Charlotte, North Carolina. Those classifying signs that told you who you were, what to do. More than those abrupt and discourteous signs one gets used to in this country—the door that says "Push," the towel dispenser that says "Press," the traffic light that says "No"—these signs were not just arrogant, they were malevolent: "White Only," "Colored Only," or perhaps just "Colored," permanently carved into the granite over a drinking fountain. But there was one set of signs that was not malevolent; it was, in fact, rather reassuring in its accuracy and fine distinctions: the pair that said "White Ladies" and "Colored Women."

The difference between white and black females seemed to me an eminently satisfactory one. White females were *ladies,* said the sign maker, worthy of respect. And the quality that made ladyhood worthy? Softness, helplessness and modesty—which I interpreted as a willingness to let others do their labor and their thinking. Colored females, on the other hand, were *women*—unworthy of respect because they were tough, capable, independent and immodest. Now, it appears, there is a consensus that those anonymous sign makers were right all along, for there is no such thing as Ladies' Liberation. Even the word "lady" is anathema to feminists. They insist upon the "woman" label as a declaration of their rejection of all that softness, helplessness and modesty, for they see them as characteristics which served only to secure their bondage to men.

Significant as that shift in semantics is, obvious as its relationship to the black-woman concept is, it has not been followed by any immediate comradery between black and white women, nor has it precipitated any rush of black women into the various chapters of NOW. It is the *Weltanschauung* of black women that is responsible for their apparent indifference to Women's Lib, and in order to discover the nature of this view of oneself in the world, one must look very closely at the black woman herself—a difficult, inevitably doomed proposition, for if anything is true of black women, it is how consistently they have (deliberately, I suspect) defied classification.

It may not even be possible to look at those militant young girls with lids lowered in dreams of guns, those middle-class socialites with 150 pairs of shoes, those wispy girl junkies who have always been older than water, those beautiful Muslim women with their bound hair and flawless skin, those television personalities who think chic is virtue and happiness a good coiffure, those sly old women in the country with their ancient love of Jesus—and still talk about The Black Woman. It is a dangerous misconception, for it encourages lump thinking. And we are so accustomed to that in our laboratories that it seems only natural to confront all human situations, direct all human discourse, in the same way. Those who adhere to the scientific method and draw general conclusions from "representative" sampling are chagrined by the suggestion that there is any other way to arrive at truth, for they like their truth in tidy sentences that begin with "all."

In the initial confrontation with a stranger, it is never "Who are you?" but "Take me to your leader." And it is this mode of thought which has made black-white relationships in this country so hopeless. There is a horror of dealing with people one by one, each as he appears. There is safety and manageability in dealing with the leader—no matter how large or diverse the leader's constituency may be. Such generalizing may be all right for plant analysis, superb for locating carcinogens in mice, and it used to be all right as a method for dealing with schools and politics. But no one would deny that it is rapidly losing effectiveness in both those areas—precisely because it involves classifying human beings and anticipating their behavior. So it is with some trepidation that anyone should undertake to generalize about still another group. Yet something in that order is legitimate, not only because unity among minorities is a political necessity, but because, at some point, one wants to get on with the differences.

What do black women feel about Women's Lib? Distrust. It is white, therefore suspect. In spite of the fact that liberating movements in the black world have been catalysts for white feminism, too many movements and organizations have made deliberate overtures to enroll blacks and have ended up by rolling them. They don't want to be used again to help somebody gain power—a power that is carefully kept out of their hands. They look at white women and see them as the enemy—for they know that racism is not confined to white men, and that there are more white women than men in this country, and that 53 percent of the population sustained an eloquent silence during times of greatest stress. The faces of those white women hovering behind that black girl at the Little Rock school in 1957 do not soon leave the retina of the mind.

When she was interviewed by Nikki Giovanni last May in *Essence* magazine, Ida Lewis, the former editor-in-chief of *Essence,* was asked why black women were not more involved in Women's Lib, and she replied: "The Women's Liberation Movement is basically a family quarrel between white women and white men. And on general principles, it's not good to get involved in family disputes. Outsiders always get shafted when the dust settles. On the other hand, I must support some of the goals [equal pay, child-care centers, etc.]. . . . But if we speak of a liberation movement, as a black woman I view my role from a black perspective—the role of black women is to continue the struggle in concert with black men for the liberation and self-determination of blacks. White power was not created to protect and preserve us as women. Nor can we view ourselves as simply American women. We are black women, and as such we must deal effectively in the black community."

To which Miss Giovanni sighed: "Well, I'm glad you didn't come out of that Women's Lib or black-man bag as if they were the alternatives. . . ."

Miss Lewis: "Suppose the Lib movement succeeds. It will follow, since white power is the order of the day, that white women will be the first hired, which will still leave black men and women outside. . . ."

It is an interesting exchange, Miss Lewis expressing suspicion and identifying closely with black men, Miss Giovanni suggesting that the two are not necessarily mutually exclusive.

But there is not only the question of color, there is the question of the color of experience. Black women are not convinced that Women's

Lib serves their best interest or that it can cope with the uniqueness of their experience, which is itself an alienating factor. The early image of Women's Lib was of an élitist organization made up of upper-middle-class women with the concerns of that class (the percentage of women in professional fields, etc.) and not paying much attention to the problems of most black women, which are not in getting into the labor force but in being upgraded in it, not in getting into medical school but in getting adult education, not in how to exercise freedom from the "head of the house" but in how to *be* head of the household.

Black women are different from white women because they view themselves differently, are viewed differently and lead a different kind of life. Describing this difference is the objective of several black women writers and scholars. But even without this newly surfacing analysis, we can gain some understanding of the black women's world by examining archetypes. The archetypes created by women about themselves are rare, and even those few that do exist may be the result of a female mind completely controlled by male-type thinking. No matter. The most unflattering stereotypes that male minds have concocted about black women contain, under the stupidity and the hostility, the sweet smell of truth.

Look, for example, at Geraldine and Sapphire—Geraldine, that campy character in Flip Wilson's comic repertory, and Sapphire, the wife of Kingfish in the *Amos and Andy* radio and TV series. Unlike Nefertiti, an archetype that black women have appropriated for themselves, Geraldine and Sapphire are the comic creations of men. Nefertiti, the romantic black queen with the enviable neck, is particularly appealing to young black women, mainly because she existed (and there are few admirable heroines in our culture), was a great beauty and is remote enough to be worshiped. There is a lot of talk about Sojourner Truth, the freed slave who preached emancipation and women's rights, but there is a desperate love for Nefertiti, simply because she was so pretty.

I suppose at bottom we are all beautiful queens, but for the moment it is perhaps just as well to remain useful women. One wonders if Nefertiti could have lasted ten minutes in a welfare office, in a Mississippi gas station, at a Parent Association meeting or on the church congregation's Stewardess Board No. 2. And since black women have to endure, that romanticism seems a needless *cul de sac,* an opiate that appears to make life livable if not serene but eventually must separate us from reality. I maintain that black women are already O.K. O.K. with our short necks. O.K. with our callused hands. O.K. with our tired feet and paper bags on the Long Island Rail Road. O.K. O.K. O.K.

As for Geraldine, her particular horror lies in her essential accuracy. Like any stereotype she is a gross distortion of reality and as such highly offensive to many black women and endearing to many whites. A single set of characteristics provokes both hatred and affection. Geraldine is defensive, cunning, sexy, egocentric and transvestite. But that's not all she is. A shift in semantics and we find the accuracy: for defensive read survivalist; for cunning read clever; for sexy read a natural unembarrassed acceptance of her sexuality; for egocentric read keen awareness of individuality; for transvestite (man in woman's dress) read a masculine strength beneath the accouterments of glamour.

Geraldine is offensive to many blacks precisely because the virtues of black women are construed in her portrait as vices. The strengths are portrayed as weaknesses—hilarious weaknesses. Yet one senses even in the laughter some awe and respect. Interestingly enough, Geraldine is absolutely faithful to one man, Killer, whom one day we may also see as caricature.

Sapphire, a name of opprobrium black men use for the nagging black wife, is also important, for in that marriage, disastrous as it was, Sapphire worked, fussed, worked and fussed, but (and this is crucial) Kingfish did whatever he pleased. Whatever. Whether he was free or irresponsible, anarchist or victim depends on your point of view. Contrary to the black-woman-as-emasculator theory, we see, even in these unflattering caricatures, the very opposite of a henpecked husband and emasculating wife—a wife who never did, and never could, manipulate her man. Which brings us to the third reason for the suspicion black women have of Women's Lib: the serious one of the relationship between black women and black men.

There are strong similarities in the way black and white men treat women, and strong similarities in the way women of both races react. But the relationship is different in a very special way.

For years in this country there was no one for black men to vent their rage on except black women. And for years black women accepted that rage—even regarded that acceptance as their unpleasant duty. But in doing so, they frequently kicked back, and they seem never to have become the "true slave" that white women see in their own history. True, the black woman did the housework, the drudgery; true, she reared the children, often alone, but she did all of that while occupying a place on the job market, a place her mate could not get or which his pride would not let him accept. And she had nothing to fall back on: not maleness, not whiteness, not ladyhood, not anything. And out of the profound desolation of her reality she may very well have invented herself.

If she was a sexual object in the eyes of men, that was their doing. Sex was *one* of her dimensions. It had to be just one, for life required many other things of her, and it is difficult to be regarded solely as a sex object when the burden of field and fire is on your shoulders. She could cultivate her sexuality but dared not be obsessed by it. Other people may have been obsessed by it, but the circumstances of her life did not permit her to dwell on it or survive by means of its exploitation.

So she combined being a responsible person with being a female—and as a person she felt free to confront not only the world at large (the rent man, the doctor and the rest of the marketplace) but her man as well. She fought him and nagged him—but knew that you don't fight what you don't respect. (If you don't respect your man, you manipulate him, the way some parents treat children and the way white women treat their men—if they can get away with it or if they do not acquiesce entirely). And even so, the black man was calling most of the shots in the home or out of it. The black woman's "bad" relationships with him were often the result of his inability to deal with a competent and complete personality and her refusal to be anything less than that. The saving of the relationship lay in her unwillingness to feel free when her man was not free.

In a way black women have known something of the freedom white women are now beginning to crave. But oddly, freedom is only sweet when it is won. When it is forced, it is called responsibility. The black woman's needs shrank to the level of her responsibility; her man's expanded in proportion to the obstacles that prevented him from assuming his. White women, on the other hand, have had too little responsibility, white men too much. It's a wonder the sexes of either race even speak to each other.

As if that were not enough, there is also the growing rage of black women over unions of black men and white women. At one time, such unions were rare enough to be amusing or tolerated. The white woman moved with the black man into a black neighborhood, and everybody tried to deal with it. Chances are the white woman who married a black man liked it that way, for she had already made some statement about her relationship with her own race by marrying him. So there were no frictions. If a white woman had a child out of wedlock by a black man, the child was deposited with the black community, or grouped with the black orphans, which is certainly one of the reasons why lists of black foundling children are so long. (Another reason is the willingness of black women to have their children instead of aborting—and to keep them, whatever the inconvenience.)

But now, with all the declarations of independence, one of the black man's ways of defining it is to broaden his spectrum of female choices, and one consequence of his new pride is the increased attraction white women feel for him. Clearly there are more and more of these unions, for there is clearly more anger about it (talking black and sleeping white is a cliché) among black women. The explanations for this anger are frequently the easy ones: there are too few eligible men, for wars continue to shoot them up; the black woman who complains is one who would be eliminated from a contest with any good-looking woman—the complaint simply reveals her inadequacy to get a man; it is a simple case of tribal sour grapes with a dash of politics thrown in.

But no one seems to have examined this anger in the light of what black women understand about themselves. These easy explanations are obviously male. They overlook the fact that the hostility comes from both popular beauties and happily married black women. There is something else in this anger, and I think it lies in the fact that black women have always considered themselves superior to white women. Not racially superior, just superior in terms of their ability to function healthily in the world.

Black women have been able to envy white women (their looks, their easy life, the attention they seem to get from their men); they could fear them (for the economic control they have had over black women's lives) and even love them (as mammies and domestic workers can); but black women have found it impossible to respect white women. I mean they never had what black men have had for white men—a feeling of awe at their accomplishments. Black women have no abiding admiration of white women as competent, complete people. Whether vying with them for the few professional slots available to women in general, or moving their dirt from one place to another, they regarded them as willful children, pretty children, mean children, ugly children, but never as real adults capable of handling the real problems of the world.

White women were ignorant of the facts of life—perhaps by choice, perhaps with the assistance of men, but ignorant anyway. They were totally dependent on marriage or male support (emotionally or economically). They confronted their sexuality with furtiveness, complete abandon or repression. Those who could afford it, gave over the management of the house and the rearing of children to others. (It is a source of amusement even now to black women to listen to feminists talk of liberation while somebody's nice black grandmother shoulders the daily responsibility of child rearing and floor mopping and the liberated one comes home to examine the housekeeping, correct it, and be entertained by the children. If Women's Lib needs those grandmothers to thrive, it has a serious flaw.) The one great disservice black women are guilty of (albeit not by choice) is that they are the means by which white women can escape the responsibilities of womanhood and remain children all the way to the grave.

It is this view of themselves and of white women that makes the preference of a black man for a white woman quite a crawful. The black women regard his choice as an inferior one. Over and over again one hears one question from them: "But why, when they marry white women, do they pick the raggletail ones, the silly, the giddy, the stupid, the flat nobodies of the race? Why no real women?" The answer, of course, is obvious. What would such a man who preferred white women do with a real woman? And would a white woman who is looking for black exotica ever be a complete woman?

Obviously there are black and white couples who love each other as people, and marry each other that way. (I can think of two such.) But there is so often a note of apology (if the woman is black) or bravado (if the man is) in such unions, which would hardly be necessary if the union was something other than a political effort to integrate one's emotions and therefore, symbolically, the world. And if all the black partner has to be is black and exotic, why not?

This feeling of superiority contributes to the reluctance of black women to embrace Women's Lib. That and the very important fact that black men are formidably opposed to their involvement in it— and for the most part the women understand their fears. In *The Amsterdam News*, an editor, while deploring the conditions of black political organizations, warns his readers of the consequences: "White politicians have already organized. And their organizers are even attempting to co-opt Black women into their organizational structure, which may well place Black women against Black men, that is, if the struggle for women's liberation is viewed by Black women as being above the struggle for Black liberation."

The consensus among blacks is that their first liberation has not been realized; unspoken is the conviction of black men that any more aggressiveness and "freedom" for black women would be intolerable, not to say counterrevolutionary.

There is also a contention among some black women that Women's Lib is nothing more than an attempt on the part of whites to become black without the responsibilities of being black. Certainly some of the demands of liberationists seem to rack up as our thing: common-law marriage (shacking); children out of wedlock, which is even fashionable now if you are a member of the Jet Set (if you are poor and black it is still a crime); families without men; right to work; sexual freedom; and an assumption that a woman is equal to a man.

Now we have come full circle: the morality of the welfare mother has become the avant-garde morality of the land. There is a good deal of irony in all of this. About a year ago in *The Village Voice* there was a very interesting exchange of letters. Cecil Brown was explaining to a young black woman the "reasons" for the black man's interest in white girls: a good deal about image, psychic needs and what not. The young girl answered in a rather poignant way to this effect: Yes, she said, I suppose, again, we black women have to wait, wait for the brother to get himself together—be enduring, understanding, and, yes, she thought they could do it again . . . but, in the meantime, what do we tell the children?

This woman who spoke so gently in those letters of the fate of the children may soon discover that the waiting period is over. The softness, the "she knows how to treat me" (meaning she knows how to be a cooperative slave) that black men may be looking for in white women is fading from view. If Women's Lib is about breaking the habit of genuflection, if it *is* about controlling one's own destiny, is about female independence in economic, personal and political ways, if it is indeed about working hard to become a person, knowing that one has to work hard at becoming anything, *Man* or *Woman*—and it it succeeds, then we may have a nation of white Geraldines and white Sapphires, and what on earth is Kingfish gonna do then?

The winds are changing, and when they blow, new things move. The liberation movement has moved from shrieks to shape. It is focusing itself, becoming a hard-headed power base, as the National Women's Political Caucus in Washington attested last month. Representative Shirley Chisholm was radiant: "Collectively we've come together, not as a Women's Lib group, but as a women's political movement." Fannie Lou Hamer, the Mississippi civil-rights leader, was there. Beulah Sanders, chairman of New York's Citywide Coordinating Committee of Welfare Groups, was there. They see, perhaps, something real: women talking about human rights rather than sexual rights—something other than a family quarrel, and the air is shivery with possibilities.

A Knowing So Deep

Essence 5 (May 1985): 230. Reprinted by permission of International Creative Management, Inc. Copyright © 1985 by Toni Morrison.

I think about us, black women, a lot. How many of us are battered and how many are champions. I note the strides that have replaced the tiptoe; I watch the new configurations we have given to personal relationships, wonder what shapes are forged and what merely bent. I think about the sisters no longer with us, who, in rage or contentment, left us to finish what should never have begun: a gender/racial war in which everybody would lose, if we lost, and in which everybody would win, if we won. I think about the Black women who never landed who are still swimming open-eyed in the sea. I think about those of us who did land and see how their strategies for survival became our maneuvers for power.

I know the achievements of the past are staggering in their everydayness as well as their singularity. I know the work undone is equally staggering, for it is nothing less than to alter the world in each of its parts: the distribution of money, the management of resources, the way families are nurtured, the way work is accomplished and valued, the penetration of the network that connects these parts. If each hour of every day brings fresh reasons to weep, the same hour is full of cause for congratulations: Our scholarship illuminates our past, our political astuteness brightens our future, and the ties that bind us to other women are in constant repair in order to build strength in this present, now.

I think about us, women and girls, and I want to say something worth saying to a daughter, a friend, a mother, a sister—my self. And if I were to try, it might go like this:

Dear Us:

You were the rim of the world—its beginning. Primary. In the first shadow the new sun threw, you carried inside you all there was of startled and startling life. And you were there to do it when the things of the world needed words. Before you were named, you were already naming.

Hell's twins, slavery and silence, came later. Still you were like no other. Not because you suffered more or longer, but because of what you knew and did before, during, and following that suffering. No one knew your weight until you left them to carry their own. But you knew. You said, "Excuse me, am I in the way?" knowing all the while that you were the way. You had this canny ability to shape an untenable reality, mold it, sing it, reduce it to its manageable, transforming essence, which is a knowing so deep it's like a secret. In your silence, enforced or chosen, lay not only eloquence but discourse so devastating that "civilization" could not risk engaging in it lest it lose the ground it stomped. All claims to prescience disintegrate when and where that discourse takes place. When you say "No" or "Yes" or "This and not that," change itself changes.

So the literature you live and write asks and gives no quarter. When you sculpt or paint, organize or refute, manage, teach, nourish, investigate or love, you do not blink. Your gaze, so lovingly unforgiving, stills, agitates and stills again. Wild or serene, vulnerable or steel trap; you are the touchstone by which all that is human can be measured. Porch or horizon, your sweep is grand.

You are what fashion tries to be—original and endlessly refreshing. Say what they like on Channel X, you are the news of the day. What doesn't love you has trivialized itself and must answer for that. And anybody who does not know your history doesn't know their own and must answer for that too.

You did all right, girl. Then, at the first naming, and now at the renaming. You did all right. You took the hands of the children and danced with them. You defended men who could not defend you. You turned grandparents over on their sides to freshen sheets and white pillows. You made meals from leavings, and leaving you was never a real separation because nobody needed your face to remember you by. And all along the way you had the best of company—others, we others, just like you. When you cried, I did too. When we fought, I was afraid you would break your fingernails or split a seam at the armhole of your jacket. And you made me laugh so hard the sound of it disappeared—returned, I guess, to its beginning when laughter and tears were sisters too.

There is movement in the shadow of a sun that is old now. There, just there. Coming from the rim of the world. A disturbing disturbance that is not a hawk nor stormy weather, but a dark woman, of all things. My sister, my me—rustling, like life.

Behind the Making of *The Black Book*

Black World 23 (February 1974): 86–90. Reprinted by permission of International Creative Management, Inc. Copyright © 1974 by Toni Morrison.

Being older than a lot of people, I remember when soul food was called supper, and when the complete failure in the neighborhood was not the drunk who sat in the alley, but the pimp who sat on the bannister. Society, or whoever, may have driven them both to extremes, but the drunk had responded with awesome (and manly) feats of consumption, endurance, and imagination, while the pimp had surrendered to a view of flesh-as-property identical to the one the old slave-master had. Both the drunk and the pimp lacked dignity, but one had forgotten his history.

It was a curious time, the Thirties, Forties and on, made more curious to me now because it seems to have no relation to the new Black history being propounded in the streets, in the classrooms and in the gatherings of Black people in this country. It is strongly hinted that we have come "up" from ignorance; that aside from Marcus Garvey and W. E. B. Du Bois, we were illiterate worshipers of white people; a non-reading people who understood only the spoken word and learned the little we did by molecular displacement. A people who didn't know enough, hate enough, or love enough. The assumption about our reading habits is based on the fact that few Black people had more than a few years of primary schooling and that reading at the sixth-grade level is not reading at all. (In spite of the fact that the *New York Times* is written at the sixth-grade level—most other newspapers at the fourth grade—and that going to school for Black people had nothing to do with the ability to read.) My grandfather went to school for one day: to tell the teacher he would not be back. Yet all of his adult life he read greedily, as did his uneducated friends.

The assumption about our loving white folks is based on Madame Walker's success and folksy expressions like "all that yaller gone to waste." Still I have never seen Black people so preoccupied with *the man* as I do now. It's as if all those Black children had their brains shot out just so we could wear a kente cloth bikini in "our own" magazine (that looks just like "his" magazine).

It is also strongly hinted that we have some special soul—some magic blacker than everybody else's and more mysterious. I have noticed that soul is always happily given over to the wretched. (Witness the great Russian soul everybody talked about during the time that nine out of eleven of them were serfs.) Soul is what the master allows you when you don't have anything else.

What I am suggesting is that there is a quality of the mystic and the reactionary in our new version of history that troubles me. I don't believe it. Do we really have to go back to Shongo and the university of Timbuktu to find some reason for going on with life? Is the far and misty past really helpful—or just a way to escape and transcend the awful reality of this day. Compared with some aspects of contemporary Black Studies, the Black Church comes off as the most pragmatic and realistic institution we ever had. (Where, for instance, could a person go to scream out his grief among people he trusted and not be embarrassed except in a church? Now the white

fashion is primal scream therapy and "contact" psychiatry. Even voo-
doo never focused on transcendental states just for the sake of being transported. It had always to do with how to get some money,
how to keep somebody from bugging you, how to get a job—the
real world.) This is not a criticism of the idea of Black Studies, but it
is a criticism of the *cul de sac* many of the courses are headed for. Of
course *The Death of Chaka* is more important than *Julius Caesar:* but
not because Chaka was Black or because he lived so long ago. His
life was more complex, more moral, and his problems have more to
do with mine.

Let me explain what I mean about mysticism and reactionaryism.
A few years ago we were called upon to make new myths, to forge a
new cosmology to live by; the assumption being either that we had
no Afro-American myths, or that if we did they were inferior. So we
skipped over some 300 to 2,000 years of lived life to find a myth to
our liking, or we made some up. Mostly we made some up. To deliberately create a myth is a contradiction in terms. A myth is whatever
concept of truth or reality a whole people has arrived at over years
of observation. It cannot be manufactured by a handful of people.
It must be the collective creation of—and acceptance by—hordes of
anonymous people. All the artists and intellectuals can do is record
it—they can't make it. To make a myth and hand it to the people
is simple propaganda. The difference between Hitler and Leadbelly.

So much Black history and art is not reinterpretation or re-
evaluation as it should be, but an attempt to defend a new idea or
destroy an old one. The excuse has been that "white" history and art
do precisely that—for *them*. Why does ours have to be better? Well,
it doesn't *have* to be any better, it just seems that we would want it
to be. Because our children can't use and don't need and will certainly reject history-as-imagined, they deserve better: history as life

lived. And there is not an artist in the world who has improved on one life lived by any Black person in the universe.

Historians must necessarily speak in generalities and must examine recorded sources: statistics on income earned, books by activists and leaders, dates, etc. . . . They habitually leave out life lived by everyday people. History for them is what great men have done. But artists don't have any such limitation, and as the truest of historians they are obligated not to. They can go ahead and say that Rosetta Tharpe could always pull more audiences than Billie Holiday; they don't have to rely on the eloquence of Frederick Douglass who spoke good nineteenth-century English. The artist can think about the fact that the Wolof word for all right is pronounced "yaw kay"— OK?; or that in the same language the word for "having one's eyes open; to be aware" is "hipi"—hip? Well, maybe the artist would not know that because the point was to have Black Studies offer African languages, not to actually study them. Offering those "mysterious" languages had, again, something to do with our magic, and something to do with reacting to the white languages of France, England, or wherever.

The best example of instant and reactionary myth-making can be found in the slogan "Black Is Beautiful." One was immediately tempted to say, "So what?" Of course, young people loved it—beauty, physical beauty, was important to them (like being "popular" in school). After all, they had grown up with Marilyn, Miss America and *Mademoiselle*. Older people liked it too, for it seemed to liberate them from the fretful problems of hair and Nadinola. But most of all white people loved it because, at last, somebody had said aloud what they had worked so hard to hide: their overwhelming attraction to us. Still, other than this brief foray into self-congratulation, that slogan didn't help us any more than that other myth of beauty helped Narcissus. You will recall that he fell in love with his reflection and pined away into death at the lip of a pool—while the world went on.

When the strength of a race depends on its beauty, when the focus is turned to how one looks as opposed to what one is, we are in trouble. I remember a white man saying to me that the killing of so many Vietnamese was "of course wrong, but worse was the fact they are so beautiful." I don't know if I loved doing the book. And, like the race, it drove me to distraction. But it was a true labor of love. Black people from all over helped with it, called about things to put in it. And, as of this writing, nobody has seen all of it together but me, the designer, the production man (who is Black) and the printer (who is Black). All the other publishing ventures I was involved in got secondary treatment because of that book. I was scared that the world would fall away before somebody put together a thing that got close to the way we really were.

Rediscovering Black History

Review of *The Black Book. New York Times Magazine* (11 August 1974): 14+. Reprinted by permission of International Creative Management, Inc. Copyright © 1974 by Toni Morrison.

In 1963, when the N.A.A.C.P. secured the old Morrison Hotel in Chicago for its annual national convention, one of that organization's demands was the removal of two statuettes of black jockeys standing in the lobby. The hotel management reluctantly agreed, but before the statuettes could be temporarily removed, they were draped with sheets. Their eyes were veiled, the jaunty caps were shrouded, those sassy hip-twists hidden. No longer would those baleful faces offend the sensibilities of blacks or encourage the contempt of whites.

Of the black people who learned of that incident, some of us were pleased by the N.A.A.C.P.'s position and the implications of its demand; some of us were amused; others startled. What on earth did little statues of black jockeys have to do with the civil-rights movement? Had those of us who admired them, or were indifferent to them, betrayed our cause? If so, then there were a host of other betrayals we were guilty of: Many dark valleys of unraised consciousness dotted our perceptions. We had laughed ourselves to tears, for example, watching the *Amos 'n' Andy* show on television. Sapphire, Kingfish, Calhoun and Mamma were not hideous stereotypes but "characters" for whom we had much affection. Yet like the jockeys in the Morrison Hotel, they disappeared at the insistence of knowl-edgeable Negroes who represented us out there in the white world. And if enjoying Kingfish was shameful, to have loved *Little Black Sambo* as a child—to have, as a matter of fact, found it the only joy-ful, noncaricatured black children's story in print—was nothing less than treason. Mumbo. Jumbo. Sambo. They were beautiful names—the kind you could whisper to a leaf or shout in the cellar and feel as though you had let something important fly from your mouth. But in the mouths of white people, the names meant something cruel. So Sambo was slaughtered, just as Amos and Andy were annihi-lated, just as the black jockeys were draped. All because of what *they thought* rather than what *we knew.*

It was precisely in that spirit of reacting to white values that later, when Civil Rights became Black Power, we came up with the slogan "Black Is Beautiful"—an accurate but wholly irrelevant observation if ever there was one. Aside from getting rid of the nagging problems of hair straighteners and Nadinola bleaching cream, aside from of-fering some relief to the difficulties of puberty (during which look-ing good and being popular are seemingly the only preoccupations), the slogan provided a psychic crutch for the needy and a second (or first) glance from whites. Regardless of those questionable comforts, the phrase was nevertheless a full confession that white definitions were important to us (having to counteract them meant they were significant) and that the quest for physical beauty was both a good and worthwhile pursuit. The implication was that once we had con-vinced everybody, including ourselves, of our beauty, then, *then . . .* what? Things would change? We could assert ourselves? Make de-mands? White people presumably had no objection to killing beau-tiful people.

But the more disturbing aspect of "Black Is Beautiful" was avoided:

When the strength of a people rests on its beauty, when the focus is on how one looks rather than what one is, we are in trouble. When we are urged to confuse dignity with prettiness, and presence with image, we are being distracted from what *is* worthy about us: for example, our intelligence, our resilience, our skill, our tenacity, irony or spiritual health. And in that absolute fit of reacting to white values, we may very well have removed the patient's heart in order to improve his complexion.

During those intense years, one felt both excitement and a sense of loss. In the push toward middle-class respectability, we wanted tongue depressors sticking from every black man's coat pocket and briefcases swinging from every black hand. In the legitimate and necessary drive for better jobs and housing, we abandoned the past and a lot of the truth and sustenance that went with it. And when Civil Rights became Black Power, we frequently chose exoticism over reality. The old verities that made being black and alive in this country the most dynamite existence imaginable—so much of what was satisfying, challenging and simply more interesting—were being driven underground—by blacks. We felt that no one was taking us seriously enough, and seriousness was what we were about in the late fifties and early sixties. In trying to cure the cancer of slavery and its consequences, some healthy as well as malignant cells were destroyed. Instead of being delighted that the profession of being a jockey virtually belonged to black men before 1900; that fourteen of the first twenty-seven Kentucky Derby races were won by black jockeys; that Isaac Murphy, a black jockey, was the first to win three Derbys; that Jimmy Lee won all six races at Churchill Downs in 1907—we draped the figures and hid their glory not only from white eyes but from our own eyes. Instead of relishing the black family portrayed in *Little Black Sambo* (a child as deeply loved and pampered by his parents as ever lived) and creating other black children's stories, we banned the hybrid one and allowed color to be added to the flesh of those illustrations in white-middle-class-oriented textbooks. Instead of killing off *Amos 'n' Andy* in 1954, we could have supported that one genuinely funny TV show and not have waited nearly two decades for *Sanford and Son*. Political expediency ran roughshod over some valuable and tender roots.

Much of that early hysteria has abated now, but there is still a strong trace of escapism and mysticism (if not plain propaganda) being taught in many black-studies classes. The one major solace has been that the masses of black people (the so-called "uneducated" ones) seem to have consistently resisted that incredible view of life through smoked glasses. The point is not to soak in some warm bath of nostalgia about the good old days—*there were none!*—but to recognize and rescue those qualities of resistance, excellence and integrity that were so much a part of our past and so useful to us and to the generations of blacks now growing up.

For larger and larger numbers of black people, this sense of loss has grown, and the deeper the conviction that something valuable is slipping away from us, the more necessary it has become to find some way to hold on to the useful past without blocking off the possibilities of the future. To create something that might last, that would bear witness to the quality and variety of black life before it became the topic of every Ph.D. dissertation and the focal point of all the mindlessness that seems to have joined the smog of California's movie world. Whatever that "something" was, it would have to be honest, would have to be rendered through our own collective consciousness. It would have to assume that we were still tough, and that our egos were not threads of jelly in constant need of glue.

Because of the work I do, my thoughts turned naturally to a book. But a book with a difference. We called it *The Black Book*.

Like every other book, it would be confined by a cover and limited to type. Nevertheless, it had to have—for want of a better word— a sound, a very special sound. A sound made up of all the elements that distinguished black life (its peculiar brand of irony, oppression, versatility, madness, joy, strength, shame, honor, triumph, grace and stillness) as well as those qualities that identified it with all of man-kind (compassion, anger, foolishness, courage, self-deception and vi-sion). And it must concentrate on life as lived—not as imagined—by the people: the anonymous men and women who speak in conven-tional histories only through their leaders. The people who had al-ways been viewed only as percentages would come alive in *The Black Book.*

Clearly, it was not a book to be put together by writers. What was needed were collectors—people who had the original raw material documenting our life: posters, letters, newspapers, advertising cards, sheet music, photographs, movie frames, books, artifacts and me-mentos. Moreover, when we needed material not in print, we would ask people for their recollections.

A friend introduced me to Middleton (Spike) Harris, who became the chief author of the project. His collection of black memorabilia is extensive and his passion for the subject as intense as it is thor-ough. Spike, a retired city employe, is well-known among black col-lectors, but his special gift is his humor, his love and his ruthlessness in his pursuit of material. His friend Morris Levitt, a retired public-school teacher and amateur black sports enthusiast, joined Harris on the project. So did Roger Furman, an actor and director of New York's black New Heritage Repertory Theater. Finally, Ernest Smith, owner of a resort on Lake George, also joined. Ernie has been a collector of black memorabilia since he was fourteen. All of these men have one thing in common: an intense love for black expression and a zest wholly free of academic careerism. These authors, a Random House designer named Jack Ribik, a production manager named Dean Ragland and I built the book, item by item, page by page, signature by signature. It was more like planting a crop than making a book, but that was precisely the spirit we wanted—an organic book which made up its own rules.

I am not sure what the project meant to the authors, but for me it was like growing up black one more time. As I worked with those men to select and focus the material, every emotion that had engulfed or buoyed me as a black in this country was repeated. It was also as though I were experiencing once again the barbarity visited upon my people as I sat in Spike Harris's apartment reading seventeenth-century through nineteenth-century newspapers with a magnifying glass:

"Flogging with a leather strap on the naked body is common; also, paddling the body with a hand-saw until the skin is a mass of blisters, and then breaking the blisters with the teeth of the saw. . . . Another method of punishment, which is inflicted for the higher order of crimes, such as running away, or other refractory conduct, is to dig a hole in the ground large enough for a slave to squat or lie down in. The victim is then stripped naked and placed in the hole, and a covering or grating of green sticks is laid over the opening. Upon this a quick fire is built, and the live embers sifted through to the naked flesh of the slave, until his body is blistered and swollen almost to bursting. . . ."

I also lived through a despair quite new to me but so deep it had no passion at all and elicited no tears. In 1856, an article, titled "A

Visit to the Slave Mother Who Killed Her Child," appeared in a publication called *The American Baptist:*

"She said that when the officers and slave-holders came to the house in which they were concealed, she caught a shovel and struck two of her children on the head, and then took a knife and cut the throat of the third, and tried to kill the other—that if they had given her time, she would have killed them all—that with regard to herself, she cared but little; but she was unwilling to have her children suffer as she had done.

"I inquired if she was not excited almost to madness when she committed the act. No, she replied, I was as cool as I now am; and would much rather kill them at once, and thus end their sufferings, than have them taken back to slavery, and be murdered by piecemeal."

Such accounts jammed the pages of early American newspapers, and once again the withering anger caused by stories of lynchings in the thirties and castrations of black veterans in the forties were made bearable only by a close examination of those who committed the crimes. Thus it became important to include data in *The Black Book* on the white society in which such psychotic phenomena occurred:

"Notice is hereby given that all the cells in this institution [the lunatic asylum in Williamburg] are occupied and that no more patients will be received. . . ."

Or: "John Newton, captain of a slave trading vessel, read the Bible daily. On board the ship with hundreds of human souls in the hold, he pursued his studies for the ministry and held prayer service on deck twice daily. He wrote a hymn: 'How Sweet the Name of Jesus Sounds.'"

In the eighteen-sixties, there was a remarkable newspaper, *The*

New York Caucasian—remarkable not only because of its existence but because it seemed to me the true result of the eighteenth century's Age of Enlightenment: the enlightenment of a few based on the dark oppression of many. The *raison d'etre* or motto for this newspaper was a remark made by Stephen A. Douglas: "I hold that this Government was made on the WHITE BASIS, by WHITE MEN, for the Benefit of WHITE MEN and THEIR POSTERITY FOREVER."

I wondered if young blacks, so quick to holler "Tom," so anxious to "off" anybody old enough to remember the great comedian Mantan Moreland, really knew what life was like in those days. I wondered if they knew the complicated psychic power one had to exercise to resist devastation. William Shockley's theories in 1974 do shock us. But imagine seeing the 1901 book *Is the Negro a Beast?* advertised today in any metropolitan daily. After examining that book, written by a William G. Schell and published by the Gospel Trumpet Publishing Co., we believed it was important to document the routine bestiality of those who had founded and settled this country:

"The simple fact of the matter is that the penal laws of England at that time [mid-eighteenth century] and for 70 years after were a black disgrace to civilization. Women and children were hanged for shoplifting to the value of a pocket-handkerchief. . . ."

Well actually there was very little comfort in recognizing the existence of such staggering ignorance and cruelty—none whatsoever, for instance, in examining the cretinous and silly faces of those men surrounding the charred corpse of the black man they had lynched. Nothing mollified the constant assault of seeing oneself in ugly caricature. The "coon" cards, trading cards, advertisements and music sheet covers that depicted us if not close to the title of Schell's book, then just a chromosome away, still mortify and enrage.

Far more interesting than our "Black is Beautiful" is this determination on the part of white people to insist on our ugliness. It never seemed a requisite of any other slave-holding society, each of which seemed quite prepared to recognize the handsomeness of their human property without the least intention of relinquishing rights over their lives. Once I heard a white man comment on the Vietnam war with much grief for the Vietnamese. He ended his brush with compassion by saying: "It seems all the more horrible to me because they are such beautiful people." His esthetic sensibilities were outraged far more than his morals, it seemed. I was tempted then—and now—to believe that although this country was easily capable of annihilating a "beautiful" people, the awareness of that beauty may very well have been a major cause of the subsequent national remorse. Would his grief have been so obvious had the Vietnamese looked like the Congolese?

A good deal of time and energy were spent during the nineteenth century proving that black people deserved to be slaves. Not the least of which effort was in the representation of blacks to children as funny, but barely verbal, animals—which is so chillingly displayed in the book *The Funny Little Darkies*. This book, published in the early nineteen-hundreds, intensified the dumbfoundedness I had always felt when considering how careless white people were of what they were admitting about themselves. Surely they knew that intelligence was judged by the ability to tell the difference between one thing and another. Surely they knew that intellect itself was the skill in determining the difference between one blood cell and another, between one molecule and another, between one leaf and another. That the finer the distinctions, the higher the intellect. The inability, then, to tell one black person from another was tantamount to a public admission of brain damage.

A brilliant example of this Gothic ignorance, which made dealing with white mentality so hopeless, appears in a letter written to W. E. B. Du Bois by a white professor:

"We are pursuing an investigation here on the subject of crying as an expression of the emotions, and should like very much to learn about its peculiarities among the colored people. We have been referred to you as a person competent to give us information on the subject.

"We desire especially to know about the following salient aspects:

"1. Whether the Negro sheds tears . . ."

That was in 1905. Since then, no group in the world has had more money spent on it to have its genetics examined, its fecundity stopped, its intelligence measured. (Who are these people who know our sperm count but not our names?) Yet despite years, despite decades of such academic energy, there is very little scholarly recognition that a major part of American history is the history of black people: how they influenced whites and how whites influenced them. There are very few examinations of U.S. economics as the growth of a country that had generations of free labor to assure that growth. Or of the legal history of this country as primarily the efforts of the courts to contain blacks. Nor is there much notice paid to the fact that anthropology is pretty much limited to the study of the black peoples of the world. Not only are white historians and social scientists uninterested in examining their own poor, they seem never to consider directing their probes to the incidents of incest or bastardy among the rich.

Just as psychiatrists are unwilling to tell a patient deranged by racism that his illness originates in the society rather than in his subconscious, so it is quite natural for Robert William Fogel and Stanley L. Engerman to choose blacks as a problem for their computers. In their new and controversial economic interpretation of slavery, *Time on the*

Cross, the economists suggest, among other things, that the evils of slavery were not as terrible as historians have insisted that the diet of slaves, after all, sometimes exceeded nineteenth-century standards of nutrition, that the life expectancy of the slave was higher than that of the white urban dweller and that only a few slaves were separated from their families and sold on the auction block. The Peculiar Institution, we are told, was evil yet certainly not *that* evil— a conclusion which suggests that Fogel and Engerman come right out of the tradition that produced that "scholar" who asked Du Bois if black people could cry.

On the other hand, we were not, as stereotype would have it, a lazy shiftless lot but an efficient people, according to Fogel and Engerman. However, no black person who ever looked at the economic growth of the nineteenth-century American South ever doubted that slaves were efficient. What is interesting is that such a conclusion is now necessary to convince white people.

Black behavior, then, has often been fascinating to "scholars" whose various studies about us are almost always silly generalizations about the whole race. If sociologists applied the same values to Ulysses (that classic absent father) as they do to black families, Penelope, a welfare mother, would have been damned for not getting a job, while Telemachus would have been persecuted in school as a product of a broken home and tracked into a class for slow readers with social adjustment problems.

In spite of this tendency to have one set of rules for black history and another for white history, I was, in completing the editing of *The Black Book,* overwhelmed with the connecting tissue between black and white history. The connection, however, was not a simple one of white oppressor and black victim. For *The New York Caucasian,* that eighteen-sixties newspaper, is as much a part of American

history as the *Colored American* publication. The white man branded
for helping slaves escape is as important to the American past as the
editor of *The Funny Little Darkies*. The Jewish hospital that opened
its doors to the black wounded during the Civil War Draft Riots is
as significant as Sydenham Hospital, which closed its doors to W. C.
Handy's wife (she died on its steps).

The two histories merge in the book, as in life, in a noon heat of
brutality and compassion, outrage and satisfaction. Thus, it was that
very mix that made editing the book so painful. Yet, as the book suggests, pain, anger, befuddlement, melancholy and despair were not—
are not—the only emotions defining the lives of black people in this
country. In fact, the real excitement of working on the book lay precisely in those areas which had nothing at all to do with despair.

There was a time when soul food was called supper, when black
men laughed at pimps as failed men, when violent crime was the
white man's thing, when we did not need a leader to tell us when
to spit (Rosa Parks, as a friend of mine once said, did not ask Martin
Luther King whether or not she should stay in her seat). There was a
time, heretical as it sounds, when we knew who we were. One could
see that knowledge, that coherence in our wide-spirited celebration
of life and our infinite tolerance of differences. We thought little
about "unity" because we loved those differences among us. Yet we
had rent parties that were truer manifestations of community love
and sharing than any slogan ever invented for us. We knew nothing of Head Start programs, yet we were admirably suited to raise
white leaders during their most formative years. Black women bore
no malice toward those children whom they loved as much as their
own progeny. Consider, for example, the origin of a popular lullaby.
A black woman is taking care of a white child, efficiently, tenderly.

Because it is a child. She has children of her own, and knows the need. So she sings it to sleep:

Hushaby, don't you cry,
Go to sleepy, little baby.
When you wake,
You shall have cake . . .

Her thoughts, however, are elsewhere—on her own child, whom she must neglect. She quietly adds a riveting verse for her own:

Way down yonder in the meadow
There's a poor little lambie
The bees and the butterflies
Pickin' out his eyes
The poor little thing cries,
"Mammy."

Yet the black mother-mammy continues to rock the white baby knowing she may one day have to defend herself against that child who could grow up to *beat* her bloody.

Nor was our psychic condition so mauled we were not capable of irony. When a Colonel Anderson located his runaway slave, he wrote to him, begging him to return. The slave, Jourdan, replied:

"Mandy [Jourdan's wife] says she would be afraid to go back without some proof that you are disposed to treat us justly and kindly—and we have concluded to test your sincerity by asking you to send us our wages for the times we served you. . . . I served you faithfully for 32 years and Mandy 20 years. At $25 a month for me and $2 a week for Mandy, our earnings would amount to $11,680. Add to this the interest for the time our wages have been kept back and deduct what you paid for our clothing and three doctor's visits to me, and pulling a tooth for Mandy, and the balance will show what we are in justice entitled to. . . . If you fail to pay us for faithful labors in the past, we can have little faith in your promises in the future. . . .

"From your old servant,

"JOURDAN ANDERSON

"P.S. Say howdy to George Carter and thank him for taking the pistol from you when you were shooting at me."

Before black life rearranged itself into elusive symbols of dashikis, pimp hats and kentecloth bikinis, we had a hold on life, an attitude which was most dramatically expressed in one particular area. This attitude was so strong and so familiar it never seemed to need definition—or never needed it until now when its death seems right at hand. It concerned work and the way we worked. There was a press toward excellence in the execution of just about everything we tackled. I don't mean the will to "make it," although there was that, too. Nor do I mean the spine-breaking labor required by overseers. I mean the pride in work done well for its own sake, something the dumb little junkies will never know. Perhaps doing a good job these days is too much like pleasing the enemy. But at one time it was different. I remember when black people refused to let the enemy— "the man"—get to them, down there, in that private place where we lived and where we exercised skill and power, be it over biscuit dough or quilts, railroads or levees, architecture or baskets. That was the whole point. White people never got to us *there*. For the relationship between a person and his work was private, because if they—the white people—killed that pride of accomplishment, little of anything else would be left. So the quilts were carefully done, since the development of a pattern was challenging, demanding and rewarding. The wrought-iron gates and balconies were made beautiful to behold. The plaster work was exquisitely decorated. Even the dolls made for the white children who were our charges were done with special care and love for the thing itself. It didn't make any difference who owned the work, the worker knew he owned it, because he had done it. Whether by sheer strength, delicacy or ingenuity, when we laid our hands to work, we did it well.

Looking at the fruits of that work displayed in *The Black Book*, I felt a renewal of pride I had not felt since 1941, when my parents told me stories of blacks who had invented airplanes, electricity and shoes. ("Oh, Mama," I cried, "everybody in the world must have had sense enough to wrap his feet." "I am telling you," she replied, "a Negro invented shoes.") And there it was among Spike Harris's collection of patents: the overshoe.

The airplane was also there as an airship registered in 1900 by John Pickering. And other inventions: Grant Woods's telephone system and apparatus, 1877; A. Miles's elevator, 1887; William Purvis's improved fountain pen, 1890; J. H. Smith's lawn sprinkler, 1897; L. S. Bailey's folding bed, 1899; W. Johnson's egg beater, 1884; C. B. Brooks's street sweeper, 1896; Burridge's and Marshman's improvement on the typewriting machine, 1885; A. L. Lewis's window cleaner, 1892; and H. L. Jones's corn harvester, 1890.

Just as it is interesting to speculate on what Africa might have become had it been allowed to develop without the rapacity of the West, it is wondrous to speculate on what black Americans might have been had we moved along at the rate and in the direction we seemed to be going in New York in the sixteen-hundreds. During that time, the Dutch had given large tracts of land to blacks of various homelands and descriptions. The first land grant in Brooklyn was issued by Dutch Governor Willem Kieft on May 27, 1643, to a black man named Antonie Jansen Van Salee. Annie d'Angola, a black woman, once owned the land on which Madison Square Garden now stands. Francisco Negro owned land in Bushwick in 1633, three years earlier than any white man's acquisition of land there.

Not even the scourge of slavery stopped black enterprise. A black woman introduced the silk industry to Alabama. O. A. Brownson wrote a text on chess. A black doctor named Daniel Williams performed open-heart surgery in 1893. Thomas Downing, who owned land on Wall Street, among other places, advanced a loan to J. G. Bennett to keep his *New York Herald* from bankruptcy.

Finally, in this long trek through three hundred years of black life, there was joy, which is what I mostly remember. The part of our lives that was spent neither on our knees nor hanging from trees. The idleness of the day broken by black boys doing the hambone. Our bodies in motion at public dances that pulled black people from as far as a hundred miles away. A glorious freedom of movement in which rites of puberty were acted out on a dance floor to the sound of brass, strings and ivory. For dancing was relief and communication, control of the body and its letting go. We danced in public and alone, on the porches and in the yards. Wherever the sound found us. And, of course, there was the music. Not only the "race records" and the live bands but the shout songs and the remnants of slave jubilees.

In *The Black Book*, there is a list of an interpretation of dreams. The list is taken from an old dream book that not only explains a particular dream but reveals what number the dreamer should play. Here is an interpretation for the person who dreams of colored people:

> "This is an excellent dream for all. It promises riches and extraordinary good health. To those in business, great success. To prisoners, a speedy release; to farmers, good crops; to the brokenhearted, courage."

The Black Book is unconventional history told from the point of view of everyday people. With the whole world as its couch and white America as its pillow, it dreams of colored people. It is indeed an excellent dream.

Rootedness: The Ancestor as Foundation

In *Black Women Writers, 1950-1980*, edited by Mari Evans. New York: Anchor Doubleday, 1984. 339–45. Reprinted by permission of International Creative Management, Inc. Copyright © 1984 by Toni Morrison.

There is a conflict between public and private life, and it's a conflict that I think ought to remain a conflict. Not a problem, just a conflict. Because they are two modes of life that exist to exclude and annihilate each other. It's a conflict that should be maintained now more than ever because the social machinery of this country at this time doesn't permit harmony in a life that has both aspects. I am impressed with the story of—probably Jefferson, perhaps not, who walked home alone after the presidential inauguration. There must have been a time when an artist could be genuinely representative *of* the tribe and *in* it; when an artist could have a tribal or racial sensibility and an individual expression of it. There were spaces and places in which a single person could enter and behave as an individual within the context of the community. A small remnant of that you can see sometimes in Black churches where people shout. It is a very personal grief and a personal statement done among people you trust. Done within the context of the community, therefore safe. And while the shouter is performing some rite that is extremely subjective, the other people are performing as a community in protecting

56

that person. So you have a public and a private expression going on at the same time. To transfer that is not possible. So I just do the obvious, which is to keep my life as private as possible; not because it is all that interesting, it's just important that it be private. And then, whatever I do that is public can be done seriously.

The autobiographical form is classic in Black American or Afro-American literature because it provided an instance in which a writer could be representative, could say, "My single solitary and individual life is like the lives of the tribe; it differs in these specific ways, but it is a balanced life because it is both solitary and representative." The contemporary autobiography tends to be "how I got over—look at me—alone—let me show you how I did it." It is inimical, I think, to some of the characteristics of Black artistic expression and influence.

The label "novel" is useful in technical terms because I write prose that is longer than a short story. My sense of the novel is that it has always functioned for the class or the group that wrote it. The history of the novel as a form began when there was a new class, a middle class, to read it; it was an art form that they needed. The lower classes didn't need novels at that time because they had an art form already: they had songs, and dances, and ceremony, and gossip, and celebrations. The aristocracy didn't need it because they had the art that they had patronized, they had their own pictures painted, their own houses built, and they made sure their art separated them from the rest of the world. But when the industrial revolution began, there emerged a new class of people who were neither peasants nor aristocrats. In large measure they had no art form to tell them how to behave in this new situation. So they produced an art form: we call it the novel of manners, an art form designed to tell people something they didn't know. That is, how to behave in this new world, how to distinguish between the good guys and the bad guys. How to get married. What a good living was. What would happen if you strayed from the fold. So that early works such as *Pamela*, by Samuel Richardson, and the Jane Austen material provided social rules and explained behavior, identified outlaws, identified the people, habits, and customs that one should approve of. They were didactic in that sense. That, I think, is probably why the novel was not missed among the so-called peasant cultures. They didn't need it, because they were clear about what their responsibilities were and who and where was evil, and where was good.

But when the peasant class, or lower class, or what have you, confronts the middle class, the city, or the upper classes, they are thrown a little bit into disarray. For a long time, the art form that was healing for Black people was music. That music is no longer *exclusively* ours; we don't have exclusive rights to it. Other people sing it and play it; it is the mode of contemporary music everywhere. So another form has to take that place, and it seems to me that the novel is needed by African-Americans now in a way that it was not needed before— and it is following along the lines of the function of novels everywhere. We don't live in places where we can hear those stories anymore; parents don't sit around and tell their children those classical, mythological archetypal stories that we heard years ago. But new information has got to get out, and there are several ways to do it. One is in the novel. I regard it as a way to accomplish certain very strong functions—one being the one I just described.

It should be beautiful, and powerful, but it should also *work*. It should have something in it that enlightens; something in it that opens the door and points the way. Something in it that suggests

what the conflicts are, what the problems are. But it need not solve those problems because it is not a case study, it is not a recipe. There are things that I try to incorporate into my fiction that are directly and deliberately related to what I regard as the major character- istics of Black art, wherever it is. One of which is the ability to be both print and oral literature: to combine those two aspects so that the stories can be read in silence, of course, but one should be able to hear them as well. It should try deliberately to make you stand up and make you feel something profoundly in the same way that a Black preacher requires his congregation to speak, to join him in the sermon, to behave in a certain way, to stand up and to weep and to cry and to accede or to change and to modify—to expand on the sermon that is being delivered. In the same way that a mu- sician's music is enhanced when there is a response from the audi- ence. Now in a book, which closes, after all—it's of some importance to me to try to make that connection—to try to make that happen also. And, having at my disposal only the letters of the alphabet and some punctuation, I have to provide the places and spaces so that the reader can participate. Because it is the affective and participa- tory relationship between the artist or the speaker and the audience that is of primary importance, as it is in these other art forms that I have described.

To make the story appear oral, meandering, effortless, spoken—to have the reader *feel* the narrator without *identifying* that narrator, or hearing him or her knock about, and to have the reader work *with* the author in the construction of the book—is what's important. What is left out is as important as what is there. To describe sexual scenes in such a way that they are not clinical, not even explicit— so that the reader brings his own sexuality to the scene and thereby participates in it in a very personal way. And owns it. To construct the dialogue so that it is heard. So that there are no adverbs attached to them: "loudly," "softly," "he said menacingly." The menace should be in the sentence. To use, even formally, a chorus. The real presence of a chorus. Meaning the community or the reader at large, commenting on the action as it goes ahead.

In the books that I have written, the chorus has changed but there has always been a choral note, whether it is the "I" narrator of *Bluest Eye,* or the town functioning as a character in *Sula,* or the neighborhood and the community that responds in the two parts of town in *Solomon.* Or, as extreme as I've gotten, all of nature thinking and feeling and watching and responding to the action going on in *Tar Baby,* so that they are in the story: the trees hurt, fish are afraid, clouds report, and the bees are alarmed. Those are the ways in which I try to incorporate, into that traditional genre the novel, unorthodox novelistic characteristics—so that it is, in my view, Black, because it uses the characteristics of Black art. I am not suggesting that some of these devices have not been used before and elsewhere—only the reason why I do. I employ them as well as I can. And those are just some; I wish there were ways in which such things could be talked about in the criticism. My general disappointment in some of the criticism that my work has received has nothing to do with approval. It has something to do with the vocabulary used in order to describe these things. I don't like to find my books condemned as bad or praised as good, when that condemnation or that praise is based on criteria from other paradigms. I would much prefer that they were dismissed or embraced based on the success of their accomplishment within the culture out of which I write.

I don't regard Black literature as simply books written *by* Black people, or simply as literature written *about* Black people, or simply as literature that uses a certain mode of language in which you just sort of drop *g*'s. There is something very special and very identifiable about it and it is my struggle to *find* that elusive but identifiable style in the books. My joy is when I think that 1 have approached it; my misery is when I think I can't get there.

[There were times when I did.] I got there in several separate places when I knew it was exactly right. Most of the time in *Song of Solomon*, because of the construction of the book and the tone in which I could blend the acceptance of the supernatural and a profound rootedness in the real world at the same time with neither taking precedence over the other. It is indicative of the cosmology, the way in which Black people looked at the world. We are very practical people, very down-to-earth, even shrewd people. But within that practicality we also accepted what I suppose could be called superstition and magic, which is another way of knowing things. But to blend those two worlds together at the same time was enhancing, not limiting. And some of those things were "discredited knowledge" that Black people had; discredited only because Black people were discredited therefore what they *knew* was "discredited." And also because the press toward upward social mobility would mean to get as far away from that kind of knowledge as possible. That kind of knowledge has a very strong place in my work.

I have talked about function in that other question, and I touched a little hit on some of the other characteristics [or distinctive elements of African-American writing], one of which was oral quality, and the participation of the reader and the chorus. The only thing that I would add for this question is the presence of an ancestor; it seems to me interesting to evaluate Black literature on what the writer does with the presence of an ancestor. Which is to say a grandfather as in Ralph Ellison, or a grandmother as in Toni Cade Bambara, or a healer as in Bambara or Henry Dumas. There is always an elder there. And these ancestors are not just parents, they are sort of timeless people whose relationships to the characters are benevolent, instructive, and protective, and they provide a certain kind of wisdom.

How the Black writer responds to that presence interests me. Some of them, such as Richard Wright, had great difficulty with that ancestor. Some of them, like James Baldwin, were confounded and disturbed by the presence or absence of an ancestor. What struck me in looking at some contemporary fiction was that whether the novel took place in the city or in the country, the presence or absence of that figure determined the success or the happiness of the character. It was the absence of an ancestor that was frightening, that was threatening, and it caused huge destruction and disarray in the work itself. That the solace comes, not from the contemplation of serene nature as in a lot of mainstream white literature, nor from the regard in which the city was held as a kind of corrupt place to be. Whether the character was in Harlem or Arkansas, the point was there, this timelessness was there, this person who represented this ancestor. And it seemed to be one of those interesting aspects of the continuum in Black or African-American art, as well as some of the things I mentioned before: the deliberate effort, on the part of the artist, to get a visceral, emotional response as well as an intellectual response as he or she communicates with the audience.

The treatment of artists by the people for whom they speak is also of some interest. That is to say, when the writer is one of them, when the voice is not the separate, isolated ivory tower voice of a very different kind of person but an implied "we" in a narration. This is disturbing to people and critics who view the artist as the supreme individual. It is disturbing because there is a notion that that's what the artist is—always in confrontation with his own society, and you can see the differences in the way in which literature is interpreted. Whether or not Sula is nourished by that village depends on your view of it. I know people who believe that she was destroyed by it. My own special view is that there was no other place where she could live. She would have been destroyed by any other place; she was permitted to "be" only in that context, and no one stoned her or killed her or threw her out. Also it's difficult to see who the winners are if you are not looking at it from that point of view. When the hero returns to the fold—returns to the tribe—it is seen by certain white critics as a defeat, by others as a triumph, and that is a difference in what the *aims* of the art are.

In *Song of Solomon* Pilate is the ancestor. The difficulty that Hagar [youngest of the trio of women in that household] has is how far removed she is from the experience of her ancestor. Pilate had a dozen years of close, nurturing relationships with two males—her father and her brother. And that intimacy and support was in her and made her fierce and loving because she had that experience. Her daughter Reba had less of that and related to men in a very shallow way. Her daughter had even less of an association with men as a child, so that the progression is really a diminishing of their abilities because of the absence of men in a nourishing way in their lives. Pilate is the apogee of all that: of the best of that which is female and the best of that which is male, and that balance is disturbed if it is not nurtured, and if it is not counted on and if it is not reproduced. That is the disability we must be on guard against for the future—the female who reproduces the female who reproduces the female. You know there are a lot of people who talk about the position that men hold as of primary importance, but actually it is if we don't keep in touch with the ancestor that we are, in fact, lost.

The point of the books is that it is *our* job. When you kill the ancestor you kill yourself. I want to point out the dangers, to show that nice things don't always happen to the totally self-reliant if there is no conscious historical connection. To say, see—this is what will happen.

I don't have much to say about that [the necessity to develop a specific Black feminist model of critical inquiry] except that I think there is more danger in it than fruit, because any model of criticism or evaluation that excludes males from it is as hampered as any model of criticism of Black literature that excludes women from it. For critics, models have some function. They like to talk in terms of models and developments and so on, so maybe its of some use to them, but I suggest that even for them there is some danger in it.

If anything I do, in the way of writing novels (or whatever I write) isn't about the village or the community or about you, then it is not about anything. I am not interested in indulging myself in some private, closed exercise of my imagination that fulfills only the obligation of my personal dreams—which is to say yes, the work must be political. It must have that as its thrust. That's a perjorative term in critical circles now: if a work of art has any political influence in it, somehow it's tainted. My feeling is just the opposite: if it has none, it is tainted.

The problem comes when you find harangue passing off as art. It seems to me that the best art is political and you ought to be able to make it unquestionably political and irrevocably beautiful at the same time.

The Site of Memory

In *Inventing the Truth: The Art and Craft of Memoir,* edited by William Zinsser. Boston: Houghton Mifflin, 1987. 103–24. Reprinted by permission of International Creative Management, Inc. Copyright © 1987 by Toni Morrison.

My inclusion in a series of talks on autobiography and memoir is not entirely a misalliance. Although it's probably true that a fiction writer thinks of his or her work as alien in that company, what I have to say may suggest why I'm not completely out of place here. For one thing, I might throw into relief the differences between self-recollection (memoir) and fiction, and also some of the similarities—the places where those two crafts embrace and where that embrace is symbiotic.

But the authenticity of my presence here lies in the fact that a very large part of my own literary heritage is the autobiography. In this country the print origins of black literature (as distinguished from the oral origins) were slave narratives. These book-length narratives (autobiographies, recollections, memoirs), of which well over a hundred were published, are familiar texts to historians and students of black history. They range from the adventure-packed life of Olaudah Equiano's *The interesting Narrative of the Life of Olaudah Equiano, or Gustavus Vassa, the African, Written by Himself* (1769) to the quiet desperation of *Incidents in the Life of a Slave Girl: Written by Herself* (1861), in which Harriet Jacobs ("Linda Brent") records hiding for seven years in a room too small to stand up in; from the political savvy of Frederick Douglass's *Narrative of the Life of Frederick Douglass, an American Slave, Written by Himself* (1845) to the subtlety and modesty of Henry Bibb, whose voice, in *Life and Adventures of Henry Bibb, an American Slave, Written by Himself* (1849), is surrounded by ("loaded with" is a better phrase) documents attesting to its authenticity. Bibb is careful to note that his formal schooling (three weeks) was short, but that he was "educated in the school of adversity, whips, and chains." Born in Kentucky, he put aside his plans to escape in order to marry. But when he learned that he was the father of a slave and watched the degradation of his wife and child, he reactivated those plans.

Whatever the style and circumstances of these narratives, they were written to say principally two things. One: "This is my historical life—my singular, special example that is personal, but that also represents the race." Two: "I write this text to persuade other people—you, the reader, who is probably not black—that we are human beings worthy of God's grace and the immediate abandonment of slavery." With these two missions in mind, the narratives were clearly pointed.

In Equiano's account, the purpose is quite up-front. Born in 1745 near the Niger River and captured at the age of ten, he survived the Middle Passage, American plantation slavery, wars in Canada and the Mediterranean; learned navigation and clerking from a Quaker named Robert King, and bought his freedom at twenty-one. He lived as a free servant, traveling widely and living most of his latter life in England. Here he is speaking to the British without equivocation: "I hope to have the satisfaction of seeing the renovation of liberty and justice resting on the British government. . . . I hope and expect the

attention of gentlemen of power. . . . May the time come—at least
the speculation is to me pleasing—when the sable people shall grate-
fully commemorate the auspicious era of extensive freedom." With
typically eighteenth-century reticence he records his singular and
representative life for one purpose: to change things. In fact, he and
his co-authors *did* change things. Their works gave fuel to the fires
that abolitionists were setting everywhere.

More difficult was getting the fair appraisal of literary critics. The
writings of church martyrs and confessors are and were read for the
eloquence of their message as well as their experience of redemption,
but the American slaves' autobiographical narratives were frequently
scorned as "biased," "inflammatory" and "improbable." These attacks are particularly difficult to understand in view of the fact that
it was extremely important, as you can imagine, for the writers of
these narratives to appear as objective as possible—not to offend the
reader by being too angry, or by showing too much outrage, or by
calling the reader names. As recently as 1966, Paul Edwards, who
edited and abridged Equiano's story, praises the narrative for its refusal to be "inflammatory."

"As a rule," Edwards writes, "he [Equiano] puts no emotional
pressure on the reader other than that which the situation itself
contains—his language does not strain after our sympathy, but ex-
pects it to be given naturally and at the proper time. This quiet avoid-
ance of emotional display produces many of the best passages in the
book." Similarly, an 1836 review of Charles Bell's *Life and Adventures of a Fugitive Slave,* which appeared in the *Quarterly Anti-Slavery
Magazine,* praised Bell's account for its objectivity. "We rejoice in
the book the more, because it is not a partisan work. . . . It broaches
no theory in regard to [slavery], nor proposes any mode or time of
emancipation."

As determined as these black writers were to persuade the reader of the evil of slavery, they also complimented him by assuming his nobility of heart and his high-mindedness. They tried to summon up his finer nature in order to encourage him to employ it. They knew that their readers were the people who could make a difference in terminating slavery. Their stories—of brutality, adversity and deliverance—had great popularity in spite of critical hostility in many quarters and patronizing sympathy in others. There was a time when the hunger for "slave stories" was difficult to quiet, as sales figures show. Douglass's *Narrative* sold five thousand copies in four months; by 1847 it had sold eleven thousand copies. Equiano's book had thirty-six editions between 1789 and 1850. Moses Roper's book had ten editions from 1837 to 1856; William Wells Brown's was reprinted four times in its first year. Solomon Northrop's book sold twenty-seven thousand copies before two years had passed. A book by Josiah Henson (argued by some to be the model for the "Tom" of Harriet Beecher Stowe's *Uncle Tom's Cabin*) had a pre-publication sale of five thousand.

In addition to using their own lives to expose the horrors of slavery, they had a companion motive for their efforts. The prohibition against teaching a slave to read and write (which in many Southern states carried severe punishment) and against a slave's learning to read and write had to be scuttled at all costs. These writers knew that literacy was power. Voting, after all, was inextricably connected to the ability to read; literacy was a way of assuming and proving the "humanity" that the Constitution denied them. That is why the narratives carry the subtitle "written by himself," or "herself," and include introductions and prefaces by white sympathizers to authenticate them. Other narratives, "edited by" such well-known antislavery figures as Lydia Maria Child and John Greenleaf Whittier, contain prefaces to assure the reader how little editing was needed. A literate slave was supposed to be a contradiction in terms.

One has to remember that the climate in which they wrote reflected not only the Age of Enlightenment but its twin, born at the same time, the Age of Scientific Racism. David Hume, Immanuel Kant and Thomas Jefferson, to mention only a few, had documented their conclusions that blacks were incapable of intelligence. Frederick Douglass knew otherwise, and he wrote refutations of what Jefferson said in "Notes on the State of Virginia": "Never yet could I find that a black had uttered a thought above the level of plain narration, never see even an elementary trait of painting or sculpture." A sentence that I have always thought ought to be engraved at the door to the Rockefeller Collection of African Art. Hegel, in 1813, had said that Africans had no "history" and couldn't write in modern languages. Kant disregarded a perceptive observation by a black man by saying, "This fellow was quite black from head to foot, a clear proof that what he said was stupid."

Yet no slave society in the history of the world wrote more—or more thoughtfully—about its own enslavement. The milieu, however, dictated the purpose and the style. The narratives are instructive, moral and obviously representative. Some of them are patterned after the sentimental novel that was in vogue at the time. But whatever the level of eloquence or the form, popular taste discouraged the writers from dwelling too long or too carefully on the more sordid details of their experience. Whenever there was an unusually violent incident, or a scatological one, or something "excessive," one finds the writer taking refuge in the literary conventions of the day. "I was left in a state of distraction not to be described" (Equiano). "But let us now leave the rough usage of the field . . . and turn our attention to the less repulsive slave life as it existed in the house of my childhood" (Douglass). "I am not about to harrow the feelings of my readers by a terrific representation of the untold horrors of that fearful system of oppression. . . . It is not my purpose to descend deeply into the dark and noisome caverns of the hell of slavery" (Henry Box Brown).

Over and over, the writers pull the narrative up short with a phrase such as, "But let us drop a veil over these proceedings too terrible to relate." In shaping the experience to make it palatable to those who were in a position to alleviate it, they were silent about many things, and they "forgot" many other things. There was a careful selection of the instances that they would record and a careful rendering of those that they chose to describe. Lydia Maria Child identified the problem in her introduction to "Linda Brent's" tale of sexual abuse: "I am well aware that many will accuse me of indecorum for presenting these pages to the public; for the experiences of this intelligent and much-injured woman belong to a class which some call delicate subjects, and others indelicate. This peculiar phase of Slavery has generally been kept veiled; but the public ought to be made acquainted with its monstrous features, and I am willing to take the responsibility of presenting them with the veil drawn [aside]."

But most importantly—at least for me—there was no mention of their interior life.

For me—a writer in the last quarter of the twentieth century, not much more than a hundred years after Emancipation, a writer who is black and a woman—the exercise is very different. My job becomes how to rip that veil drawn over "proceedings too terrible to relate." The exercise is also critical for any person who is black, or who belongs to any marginalized category, for, historically, we were seldom invited to participate in the discourse even when we were its topic.

Moving that veil aside requires, therefore, certain things. First of all, I must trust my own recollections. I must also depend on the recollections of others. Thus memory weighs heavily in what I write, in how I begin and in what I find to be significant. Zora Neale Hurston said, "Like the dead-seeming cold rocks, I have memories within that came out of the material that went to make me." These "memories within" are the subsoil of my work. But memories and recollections won't give me total access to the unwritten interior life of these people. Only the act of the imagination can help me.

If writing is thinking and discovery and selection and order and meaning, it is also awe and reverence and mystery and magic. I suppose I could dispense with the last four if I were not so deadly serious about fidelity to the milieu out of which I write and in which my ancestors actually lived. Infidelity to that milieu—the absence of the interior life, the deliberate excising of it from the records that the slaves themselves told—is precisely the problem in the discourse that proceeded without us. How I gain access to that interior life is what drives me and is the part of this talk which both distinguishes my fiction from autobiographical strategies and which also embraces certain autobiographical strategies. It's a kind of literary archeology: on the basis of some information and a little bit of guesswork you journey to a site to see what remains were left behind and to reconstruct the world that these remains imply. What makes it fiction is the nature of the imaginative act: my reliance on the image— on the remains—in addition to recollection, to yield up a kind of a truth. By "image," of course, I don't mean "symbol"; I simply mean "picture" and the feelings that accompany the picture.

Fiction, by definition, is distinct from fact. Presumably it's the product of imagination—invention—and it claims the freedom to dispense with "what really happened," or where it really happened, or when it really happened, and nothing in it needs to be publicly verifiable, although much in it can be verified. By contrast, the scholarship of the biographer and the literary critic seems to us only trustworthy when the events of fiction can be traced to some publicly verifiable fact. It's the research of the "Oh, yes, this is where he or she got it from" school, which gets its own credibility from excavating the credibility of the sources of the imagination, not the nature of the imagination.

The work that I do frequently falls, in the minds of most people, into that realm of fiction called fantastic, or mythic, or magical, or unbelievable. I'm not comfortable with these labels. I consider that my single gravest responsibility (in spite of that magic) is not to lie. When I hear someone say, "Truth is stranger than fiction," I think that old chestnut is truer than we know, because it doesn't say that truth is truer than fiction; just that it's stranger, meaning that it's odd. It may be excessive, it may be more interesting, but the important thing is that it's random—and fiction is not random.

Therefore the crucial distinction for me is not the difference between fact and fiction, but the distinction between fact and truth. Because facts can exist without human intelligence, but truth cannot. So if I'm looking to find and expose a truth about the interior life of people who didn't write it (which doesn't mean that they didn't have it); if I'm trying to fill in the blanks that the slave narratives left—to part the veil that was so frequently drawn, to implement the stories that I heard—then the approach that's most productive and most trustworthy for me is the recollection that moves from the image to the text. Not from the text to the image.

Simone de Beauvoir, in *A Very Easy Death*, says, "I don't know why I was so shocked by my mother's death." When she heard her mother's name being called at the funeral by the priest, she says, "Emotion seized me by the throat. . . . 'Françoise de Beauvoir': the words brought her to life; they summed up her history, from birth to marriage to widowhood to the grave. Françoise de Beauvoir—that retiring woman, so rarely named, became an *important* person." The book becomes an exploration both into her own grief and into the images in which the grief lay buried.

Unlike Mme. de Beauvoir, Frederick Douglass asks the reader's patience for spending about half a page on the death of his grandmother—easily the most profound loss he had suffered—and he apologizes by saying, in effect, "It really was very important to me. I hope you aren't bored by my indulgence." He makes no attempt to explore that death: its images or its meaning. His narrative is as close to factual as he can make it, which leaves no room for subjective speculation. James Baldwin, on the other hand, in *Notes of a Native Son*, says, in recording his father's life and his own relationship to his father, "All of my father's Biblical texts and songs, which I had decided were meaningless, were ranged before me at his death like empty bottles, waiting to hold the meaning which life would give them for me." And then his text fills those bottles. Like Simone de Beauvoir, he moves from the event to the image that it left. My route is the reverse: the image comes first and tells me what the "memory" is about.

I can't tell you how I felt when my father died. But I was able to write *Song of Solomon* and imagine, not him, and not his specific interior life, but the world that he inhabited and the private or interior life of the people in it. And I can't tell you how I felt reading to my grandmother while she was turning over and over in her bed (because she was dying, and she was not comfortable), but I could try to reconstruct the world that she lived in. And I have suspected, more often than not, that I *know* more than she did, that I *know* more than my grandfather and my great-grandmother did, but I also know that I'm no wiser than they were. And whenever I have tried earnestly to diminish their vision and prove to myself that I know more, and when I have tried to speculate on their interior life and match it up with my own, I have been overwhelmed every time by the richness of theirs compared to my own. Like Frederick Douglass talking about his grandmother, and James Baldwin talking about his father, and Simone de Beauvoir talking about her mother, these people are my access to me; they are my entrance into my own interior life. Which is why the images that float around them—the remains, so to speak, at the archeological site—surface first, and they surface so vividly and so compellingly that I acknowledge them as my route to a re-construction of a world, to an exploration of an interior life that was not written and to the revelation of a kind of truth.

So the nature of my research begins with something as ineffable and as flexible as a dimly recalled figure, the corner of a room, a voice. I began to write my second book, which was called *Sula*, be-cause of my preoccupation with a picture of a woman and the way in which I heard her name pronounced. Her name was Hannah, and I think she was a friend of my mother's. I don't remember see-ing her very much, but what I do remember is the color around her—a kind of violet, a suffusion of something violet—and her eyes, which appeared to be half closed. But what I remember most is how the women said her name: how they said "Hannah Peace" and smiled to themselves, and there was some secret about her that they knew, which they didn't talk about, at least not in my hearing, but it seemed *loaded* in the way in which they said her name. And I suspected that she was a little bit of an outlaw but that they approved in some way.

And then, thinking about their relationship to her and the way in which they talked about her, the way in which they articulated her name, made me think about friendship between women. What is it that they forgive each other for? And what it is that is unforgivable in the world of women. I don't want to know any more about Miss Hannah Peace, and I'm not going to ask my mother who she really was and what did she do and what were you laughing about and why were you smiling? Because my experience when I do this with my mother is so crushing: she will give you *the* most pedestrian information you ever heard, and I would like to keep all of my remains and my images intact in their mystery when I begin. Later I will get to the facts. That way I can explore two worlds—the actual and the possible.

What I want to do this evening is to track an image from picture to meaning to text—a journey which appears in the novel that I'm writing now, which is called *Beloved*.

I'm trying to write a particular kind of scene, and I see corn on the cob. To "see" corn on the cob doesn't mean that it suddenly hovers; it only means that it keeps coming back. And in trying to figure out "What is all this corn doing?" I discover what it *is* doing.

I see the house where I grew up in Lorain, Ohio. My parents had a garden some distance away from our house, and they didn't welcome me and my sister there, when we were young, because we were not able to distinguish between the things that they wanted to grow and the things that they didn't, so we were not able to hoe, or weed, until much later.

I see them walking, together, away from me. I'm looking at their backs and what they're carrying in their arms: their tools, and maybe a peck basket. Sometimes when they walk away from me they hold hands, and they go to this other place in the garden. They have to cross some railroad tracks to get there.

I also am aware that my mother and father sleep at odd hours because my father works many jobs and works at night. And these naps are times of pleasure for me and my sister because nobody's giving us chores, or telling us what to do, or nagging us in any way. In addition to which, there is some feeling of pleasure in them that I'm only vaguely aware of. They're very rested when they take these naps.

And later on in the summer we have an opportunity to eat corn, which is the one plant that I can distinguish from the others, and which is the harvest that I like the best; the others are the food that no child likes—the collards, the okra, the strong, violent vegetables that I would give a great deal for now. But I do like the corn because it's sweet, and because we all sit down to eat it, and it's finger food, and it's hot, and it's even good cold, and there are neighbors in, and there are uncles in, and it's easy, and it's nice.

The picture of the corn and the nimbus of emotion surrounding it became a powerful one in the manuscript I'm now completing.

Authors arrive at text and subtext in thousands of ways, learning each time they begin anew how to recognize a valuable idea and how to render the texture that accompanies, reveals or displays it to its best advantage. The process by which this is accomplished is endlessly fascinating to me. I have always thought that as an editor for twenty years I understood writers better than their most careful critics, because in examining the manuscript in each of its subsequent stages I knew the author's process, how his or her mind worked, what was effortless, what took time, where the "solution" to a problem came from. The end result—the book—was all that the critic had to go on.

Still, for me, that was the least important aspect of the work. Because, no matter how "fictional" the account of these writers, or how much it was a product of invention, the act of imagination is bound up with memory. You know, they straightened out the Mississippi River in places, to make room for houses and livable acreage. Occasionally the river floods these places. "Floods" is the word they use, but in fact it is not flooding; it is remembering. Remembering where it used to be. All water has a perfect memory and is forever trying to get back to where it was. Writers are like that: remembering where we were, what valley we ran through, what the banks were like, the light that was there and the route back to our original place. It is emotional memory—what the nerves and the skin remember as well as how it appeared. And a rush of imagination is our "flooding."

Along with personal recollection, the matrix of the work I do is the wish to extend, fill in and complement slave autobiographical narratives. But only the matrix. What comes of all that is dictated by other concerns, not least among them the novel's own integrity. Still, like water, I remember where I was before I was "straightened out."

Q. I would like to ask about your point of view as a novelist. Is it a vision, or are you taking the part of the particular characters?

A. I try sometimes to have genuinely minor characters just walk through, like a walk-on actor. But I get easily distracted by them, because a novelist's imagination goes like that: every little road looks to me like an adventure, and once you begin to claim it and describe it, it looks like more, and you invent more and more and more. I don't mind doing that in my first draft, but afterward I have to cut back. I have seen myself get distracted, and people have loomed much larger than I had planned, and minor characters have seemed a little bit more interesting than they need to be for the purposes of the book. In that case I try to endow them: if there are little pieces of information that I want to reveal, I let them do some of the work. But I try not to get carried away; I try to restrain it, so that, finally, the texture is consistent and nothing is wasted; there are no words in the final text that are unnecessary, and no people who are not absolutely necessary.

As for the point of view, there should be the illusion that it's the characters' point of view, when in fact it isn't; it's really the narrator who is there but who doesn't make herself (in my case) known in that role. I like the feeling of a *told* story, where you hear a voice but you can't identify it, and you think it's your own voice. It's a comfortable voice, and it's a guiding voice, and it's alarmed by the same things that the reader is alarmed by, and it doesn't know what's going to happen next either. So you have this sort of guide. But that guide can't have a personality; it can only have a sound, and you have to feel comfortable with this voice, and then this voice can easily abandon itself and reveal the interior dialogue of a character. So it's a combination of using the point of view of various characters but still retaining the power to slide in and out, provided that when I'm "out" the reader doesn't see little fingers pointing to what's in the text.

What I really want is that intimacy in which the reader is under the impression that he isn't really reading this; that he is participating in it as he goes along. It's unfolding, and he's always two beats ahead of the characters and right on target.

Q. You have said that writing is a solitary activity. Do you go into steady seclusion when you're writing, so that your feelings are sort of contained, or do you have to get away, and go out shopping and . . . ?

A. I do all of it. I've been at this book for three years. I go out shopping, and I stare, and I do whatever. It goes away. Sometimes it's very intense and I walk—I mean, I write a sentence and I jump up and run outside or something; it sort of beats you up. And sometimes I don't. Sometimes I write long hours every day. I get up at 5:30 and just go do it, and if I don't like it the next day, I throw it away. But I sit down and do it. By now I know how to get to that place where something is working. I didn't always know; I thought every thought I had was interesting—because it was mine. Now I know better how to throw away things that are not useful. I can stand around and do other things and think about it at the same time. I don't mind not writing every minute; I'm not so terrified.

When you first start writing—and I think it's true for a lot of beginning writers—you're scared to death that if you don't get that sentence right that minute it's never going to show up again. And it isn't. But it doesn't matter—another one will, and it'll probably be better. And I don't mind writing badly for a couple of days because I know I can fix it—and fix it again and again and again, and it will be better. I don't have the hysteria that used to accompany some of those dazzling passages that I thought the world was just dying for me to remember. I'm a little more sanguine about it now. Because the best part of it all, the absolutely most delicious part, is finishing it and then doing it over. That's the thrill of a lifetime for me: if I can just get done with that first phase and then have infinite time to fix it and change it. I rewrite a lot, over and over again, so that it looks like I never did. I try to make it look like I never touched it, and that takes a lot of time and a lot of sweat.

Q. In Song of Solomon, *what was the relationship between your memories and what you made up? Was it very tenuous?*

A. Yes, it was tenuous. For the first time I was writing a book in which the central stage was occupied by men, and which had something to do with my loss, or my perception of loss, of a man (my father) and the world that disappeared with him. (It didn't, but I *felt* that it did.) So I was re-creating a time period that was his—not biographically his life or anything in it; I use whatever's around. But it seemed to me that there was this big void after he died, and I filled it with a book that was about men because my two previous books had had women as the central characters. So in that sense it was about my memories and the need to invent. I had to do something. I was in such a rage because my father was dead. The connections between us were threads that I either mined for a lot of strength or they were purely invention. But I created a male world and inhab-ited it and it had this quest—a journey from stupidity to epiphany, of a man, a complete man. It was my way of exploring all that, of trying to figure out what he may have known.

Writers and Writing

On Behalf of Henry Dumas

An invitation to a book party for *Play Ebony Play Ivory* and *Ark of Bones* and a book club announcement for *Jonoah and the Green Stone*. Printed in *Black American Literature Forum* 22.2 (Summer 1988): 310–12. Reprinted by permission of International Creative Management, Inc. Copyright © 1988 by Toni Morrison.

He was a genius, an absolute genius. I wish he were around now to help us straighten out the mess.

—Toni Morrison

24 April 1983

September 17, 1974

In 1968, a young Black man, Henry Dumas, went through a turnstile at a New York City subway station. A transit cop shot him in the chest and killed him. Circumstances surrounding his death remain unclear. Before that happened, however, he had written some of the most beautiful, moving, and profound poetry and fiction that I have ever in my life read. He was thirty-three years old when he was killed, but in those thirty-three years, he had completed work, the quality and quantity of which are almost never achieved in several lifetimes. He was brilliant. He was magnetic, and he was an incredible artist.

A cult has grown up around Henry Dumas—a very deserved cult.

And it is my privilege to publish a collection of both his poetry, *Play Ebony Play Ivory,* and his short stories, *Ark of Bones.* It is very difficult to do publicity for an unknown writer and much more difficult to do publicity for an unknown and no longer living writer. But we are determined to bring to the large community of Black artists and Black people in general this man's work. We are planning, therefore, to have a Book Party, and I would like very much to have your participation. I don't mean just an invitation but actually your participation. I am sending you, under separate cover, copies of Henry Dumas's work. If it is at all possible, I would like for you to read his work, choose passages you feel moved by, and join us at the book party in order to read from his work. This will be a gathering for those of us who knew him, for those of us who know his work, and for those of us who are being introduced to him. Already several people have agreed to come and read from his work: Angela Davis will read, I will read, Jayne Cortez will read, Eugene Redmond will read—and Melvin Van Peebles, John Williams, and many, many others have offered their support.

We are planning to have this commemorative book party at the Center for Inter-American Relations at 680 Park Avenue, New York City, from 6:00–9:00 p.m. on October 13. We will be calling together a number of artists and scholars to pay a meaningful tribute to this extraordinary talent. I will be grateful to you if you would agree to read. We expect, of course, a large press representation, but I don't want our gathering to lose any of its beauty because of that. Please let me know as quickly as you can, whether I can count on you.

Regards,

Toni Morrison

Editor, Random House

Spring 1976

MEMO TO: Book Clubs
FROM: Toni Morrison, Editor
SUBJECT: *Jonoah and the Green Stone* by Henry Dumas

The discovery of Henry Dumas's novel *Jonoah and the Green Stone* brought about quite a bit of excitement. When *Ark of Bones* (short stories) and *Play Ebony Play Ivory* (poetry) were published posthumously in 1974 to spectacular reviews, no one dreamed there existed a novel fulfilling the enormous promise of Dumas's briefer works.

Here, in the backwaters of Arkansas, where the Mississippi River, both treacherous and life-giving, is the central metaphor—the narrator begins his story: floating on a johnnyboat—in the middle of a flood that has just orphaned him. His name is John. And when a Black family—stranded on a roof—is saved by climbing aboard his raft—they add "Noah" to his name.

Jonoah comes to maturity amid the turbulence of the 1960s. Part showman, part conman ripping off the Civil Rights Movement in the North, Jonoah pays lip service to all groups and dues to none, until, in a scene so well written it chills the skin, Jonoah is hunted down and this time is certain he will die.

Our publication date is May and price is $7.95.

We hope you share our enthusiasm.

Preface to *Deep Sightings and Rescue Missions* by Toni Cade Bambara

From *Deep Sightings and Rescue Missions: Essays, Fiction and Conversations* by Toni Cade Bambara, edited by Erroll McDonald. New York: Pantheon Books, 1996. Reprinted in *Nation* 263 (28 October 1996): 66–67. Reprinted by permission of International Creative Management, Inc. Copyright © 1996 by Toni Morrison.

Deep Sightings and Rescue Missions is unlike other books by Toni Cade Bambara. She did not gather or organize the contents. She did not approve or choose the photograph on the jacket. She did not post a flurry of letters, notes and bulletins on the design, on this or that copy change, or to describe an innovative idea about the book's promotion. And of her books published by Random House *(Gorilla, My Love, The Seabirds Are Still Alive* and *Salt Eaters)* only this one did not have the benefit, the joy, of a series of "editorial meetings" between us. Hilarious title struggles. Cloaked suggestions for ways to highlight, to foreground. Breathless discussions about what the whores really meant. Occasional battles to locate the double meaning, the singular word. Trips uptown for fried fish. Days and days in a house on the river—she, page in hand, running downstairs to say, "Does this do it?"

Editing sometimes requires re-structuring, setting loose or nailing down; paragraphs, pages may need re-writing, sentences (especially final or opening ones) may need to be deleted or re-cast; incomplete images or thoughts may need expansion, development. Sometimes the point is buried or too worked-up. Other times the tone is "off," the voice is wrong or unforthcoming or so self-regarding it distorts or mis-shapes the characters it wishes to display. In some manuscripts traps are laid so the reader is sandbagged into focusing on the author's superior gifts or knowledge rather than the intimate, reader-personalized world fiction can summon. Virtually none of that is applicable to editing Bambara's fiction.

Her writing is woven, aware of its music, its overlapping waves of scenic action, so clearly on its way—like a magnet collecting details in its wake, each of which is essential to the final effect. Entering her prose with a red pencil must be delicate; one ill-advised (or well-advised) "correction" can dislodge a thread, unravel an intricate pattern which is deceptively uncomplicated at first glance—but only at first glance.

Bambara is a writer's writer, an editor's writer, a reader's writer. Gently but pointedly she encourages us to rethink art and public space in "The War of the Wall." She is all "eyes, sweetness and stingers" in "Luther on Sweet Auburn" and in "Baby's Breath." She is wisdom's clarity in "Going Critical," plumbing the ultimate separation for meaning as legacy.

Although her insights are multiple, her textures layered and her narrative trajectory implacable, nothing distracts from the sheer satisfaction her story-telling provides. That is a little word—satisfaction—in an environment where superlatives are as common as the work they describe. But there is no other word for the wash of recognition, the thrill of deep sight, the sheer pleasure a reader takes in the company Bambara keeps. In "Ice," for example, watching her effortlessly transform a story about responsibility into the responsibility of story-telling is pure delight and we get to be in warm and splendid company all along the way.

I don't know if she knew the heart cling of her fiction. Its pedagogy, its use, she knew very well, but I have often wondered if she knew how brilliant at it she was. There was no division in her mind between optimism and ruthless vigilance; between aesthetic obligation and the aesthetics of obligation. There was no doubt whatsoever that the work she did had work to do. She always knew what her work was for. Any hint that art was over there and politics was over here would break her up into tears of laughter, or elicit a look so withering it made silence the only intelligent response. More often she met the art/politics fake debate with a slight wave-away of the fingers on her beautiful hand, like the dismissal of a mindless, desperate fly who had maybe two little hours of life left.

Of course she knew. It's all there in "How She Came By Her Name." The ear with flawless pitch; integrity embedded in the bone; daunting artistic criteria. Perhaps my wondering whether or not she realized how original, how rare her writing is prompted by the fact that I knew it was not her only love. She had another one. Stronger. As the Essays and Conversations portion of this collection testifies, (especially after the completion of her magnum opus about the child murders in Atlanta) she came to prefer film: writing scripts, making film, critiquing, teaching, analyzing it and enabling others to do the same. *The Bombing of Osage Avenue* and *W. E. B. Du Bois: A Biography in Four Voices* contain sterling examples of her uncompromising gifts and her determination to help rescue a genre from its powerful social irrelevancy.

In fiction, in essays, in conversation one hears the purposeful quiet of this ever vocal woman; feels the tenderness in this tough

Harlem/Brooklyn girl; joins the playfulness of this profoundly serious writer. When turns of events wearied the gallant and depleted the strong, Toni Cade Bambara, her prodigious talent firmly in hand, stayed the distance.

Editing her previous work was a privilege she permitted me. Editing her posthumous work is a gift she has given me. I will miss her forever.

James Baldwin: His Voice Remembered; Life in His Language

New York Times Book Review (20 December 1987). Reprinted by permission of International Creative Management, Inc. Copyright © 1987 by Toni Morrison.

Jimmy, there is too much to think about you, and too much to feel. The difficulty is your life refuses summation—it always did—and invites contemplation instead. Like many of us left here I thought I knew you. Now I discover that in your company it is myself I know. That is the astonishing gift of your art and your friendship: You gave us ourselves to think about, to cherish. We are like Hall Montana[1] watching "with new wonder" his brother saints, knowing the song he sang is us, "He is us."

I never heard a single command from you, yet the demands you made on me, the challenges you issued to me, were nevertheless unmistakable, even if unenforced: that I work and think at the top of my form, that I stand on moral ground but know that ground must be shored up by mercy, that "the world is before [me] and [I] need not take it or leave it as it was when [I] came in."

Well, the season was always Christmas with you there and, like one aspect of that scenario, you did not neglect to bring at least three gifts. You gave me a language to dwell in, a gift so perfect it seems my own invention. I have been thinking your spoken and written thoughts for so long I believed they were mine. I have been seeing the world through your eyes for so long, I believed that clear clear view was my own. Even now, even here, I need you to tell me what I am feeling and how to articulate it. So I have pored again through the 6,895 pages of your published work to acknowledge the debt and thank you for the credit. No one possessed or inhabited language for me the way you did. You made American English honest— genuinely international. You exposed its secrets and reshaped it until it was truly modern dialogic, representative, humane. You stripped it of ease and false comfort and fake innocence and evasion and hypocrisy. And in place of deviousness was clarity. In place of soft plump lies was a lean, targeted power. In place of intellectual disingenuousness and what you called "exasperating egocentricity," you gave us undecorated truth. You replaced lumbering platitudes with an upright elegance. You went into that forbidden territory and decolonized it, "robbed it of the jewel of its naivete," and un-gated it for black people so that in your wake we could enter it, occupy it, restructure it in order to accommodate our complicated passion— not our vanities but our intricate, difficult, demanding beauty, our tragic, insistent knowledge, our lived reality, our sleek classical imagination—all the while refusing "to be defined by a language that has never been able to recognize [us]." In your hands language was handsome again. In your hands we saw how it was meant to be: neither bloodless nor bloody, and yet alive.

It infuriated some people. Those who saw the paucity of their own imagination in the two-way mirror you held up to them attacked the mirror, tried to reduce it to fragments which they could then rank and grade, tried to dismiss the shards where your image and theirs remained—locked but ready to soar. You are an artist after all and an artist is forbidden a career in this place; an artist is permitted only a commercial hit. But for thousands and thousands of those who embraced your text and who gave themselves permission to hear your language, by that very gesture they ennobled themselves, became enshrouded, civilized.

The second gift was your courage, which you let us share: the courage of one who could go as a stranger in the village and transform the distances between people into intimacy with the whole world; courage to understand that experience in ways that made it a personal revelation for each of us. It was you who gave us the courage to appropriate an alien, hostile, all-white geography because you had discovered that "this world [meaning history] is white no longer and it will never be white again." Yours was the courage to live life in and from its belly as well as beyond its edges, to see and say what it was, to recognize and identify evil but never fear or stand in awe of it. It is a courage that came from a ruthless intelligence married to a pity so profound it could convince anyone who cared to know that those who despised us "need the moral authority of their former slaves, who are the only people in the world who know anything about them and who may be, indeed, the only people in the world who really care anything about them." When that unassailable combination of mind and heart, of intellect and passion was on display it guided us through treacherous landscape as it did when you wrote these words—words every rebel, every dissident, revolutionary, every practicing artist from Capetown to Poland from Waycross to Dublin memorized: "A person does not lightly elect to oppose his society. One would much rather be at home among one's compatriots than be mocked and detested by them. And there is a level on which the mockery of the people, even their hatred, is moving, because it is so blind: It is terrible to watch people cling to their captivity and insist on their own destruction."

The third gift was hard to fathom and even harder to accept. It was your tenderness—a tenderness so delicate I thought it could not last, but last it did and envelop me it did. In the midst of anger it tapped me lightly like the child in Tish's[2] womb: "Something almost as hard to catch as a whisper in a crowded place, as light and as definite as a spider's web, strikes below my ribs, stunning and astonishing my heart . . . the baby, turning for the first time in its incredible veil of water, announces its presence and claims me; tells me, in that instant, that what can get worse can get better . . . in the meantime— forever—it is entirely up to me." Yours was a tenderness, of vulnerability, that asked everything, expected everything and, like the world's own Merlin, provided us with the ways and means to deliver. I suppose that is why I was always a bit better behaved around you, smarter, more capable, wanting to be worth the love you lavished, and wanting to be steady enough to witness the pain you had witnessed and were tough enough to bear while it broke your heart, wanting to be generous enough to join your smile with one of my own, and reckless enough to jump on in that laugh you laughed. Because our joy and our laughter were not only all right, they were necessary.

You knew, didn't you, how I needed your language and the mind that formed it? How I relied on your fierce courage to tame wildernesses for me? How strengthened I was by the certainty that came from knowing you would never hurt me? You knew, didn't you, how I loved your love? You knew. This then is no calamity. No. This is jubilee. "Our crown," you said, "has already been bought and paid for. All we have to do," you said, "is wear it."

And we do, Jimmy. You crowned us.

Notes

1. A character in Baldwin's novel *Just Above My Head.*
2. A character in Baldwin's novel *If Beale Street Could Talk.*

Speaking of Reynolds Price

In *Critical Essays on Reynolds Price*, edited by James A. Schiff. New York: G. K. Hall, 1994. 44–46. From an interview conducted on 14 May 1992, by Charles Guggenheim for his 1994 documentary film about Reynolds Price, *Clear Pictures*. Reprinted by permission of International Creative Management, Inc. Copyright © 1994 by Toni Morrison.

I have never been with Reynolds when I didn't remember it. And that's saying a lot you know, after you reach sixty. I haven't seen him all that much, but every one of the occasions in which we were together I remember; nothing has ever gotten fuzzy. . . . There's a little bit of cheater in our relationship. He laughs and he understands laughter the way I do. Which is more than mere amusement. It's controlling the reins of our imagination. And some of the things that break Reynolds up might not do the same for other people, but I will scream. He understands incredibly well a level of irony and outrage, the exaggerated moment that you cannot. But he'll also cry. I remember very clearly sitting with him in this theater, and I think we were in California for the literature panel of the National Endowment for the Arts, and we were looking at a film and I sat next to him and the film was about Native Americans. I don't remember whether it was a terribly good film, but it tried to talk about the necessity for encouraging art among young Native Americans. As a matter of fact, my distinct impression is that it wasn't a very good film, but on the screen a young boy appeared, fairly unattractive . . . and not at all appealing, just young and Native American. And he began to talk about what he thought his future might be. And it was interesting but not particularly eloquent; you know, the kind of thing you'd expect. And I felt this tremor next to me. And I looked to my right at Reynolds—tears were running unashamedly down his face. He was simply looking at that boy and knowing on some level that probably none of that would ever happen, and why it would never happen, and who knows what else. Now this was in a theater full of other writers, critics, scholars, et cetera, and he was overwhelmed in the nicest way and he was fearless and it was more than compassion. It was a kind of physically intelligent response that he made in a public sphere. And I don't know many men like that. . . .

I know a lot of his work and mostly his poetry, which is so powerful and well crafted. I don't know what his reputation is among poets. They tend to be very cliquish. But I cannot imagine his not having the strongest following and reputation among poets. His poetry is extraordinary to me. . . .

When he was recuperating in some fashion—not completely but he was able to work and move about—everything began to pour out of him. And not just volume but quality, just incredible, beautiful things, and I thought, Well, maybe it's the up-against-the-wall syndrome. The magnificent work that can somehow come out of unbelievable pressure. You think of the wonderful work that was done in the forties under Hitler in occupied France. I mean sometimes with the proximity of the end you strip away all of the weighty, vain, comfortable things that we yearn for, but can delay and distract a writer or a painter. Maybe that's it. I know I didn't begin to write young, the way Reynolds did. I was over thirty, and when I did begin to write it was because I was in a very hard place and there was nothing else to do. And it may be the same for him. I'm only speculating, but it's just amazing and delightful. He's so productive and so good at it.

Reynolds, for me, has this extraordinary combination of recklessness and discipline in some combination that is astonishing. So I see the discipline in the pedagogy and the recklessness in other aspects of his life, and in his humor and in his insight. What he sees in nature, in animals, in people is both inventive and reckless, but he reveals it with a masterful discipline of the language and the responsibilities of the language. . . .

Charles Guggenheim {director and interviewer}: One of the criticisms of Reynolds is that he puts rather eloquent, insightful dialogue in the mouths of some of his characters who are really quite simple, rather middle-class people. Some people find that hard to accept. I was curious what your reaction to that is.

Toni Morrison: I guess I know the nature of the complaint because there is the assumption—it's a funny kind of elitism—that lower- or middle-class people are functionally illiterate and don't have complicated thoughts and complicated language and complicated images. I find it just hopeless to try to persuade anybody differently, and probably one of the reasons that Reynolds and I have always loved one another is because in this area of black-white relations, having to do with the language of black people and the language of poor people who are black and white, he never patronizes his characters, you never pity those people—neither one of us does, in the text I mean. And their language is powerfully articulated, whether or not the grammar is the grammar of standard English. . . . I think its an illegitimate complaint on the part of the critics. I thought Ibsen solved all that. Or James Joyce. I mean, you can really have tragedy that belongs to people who are not in the so-called aristocracy or the upper class. It's amazing that anybody would still level that kind of charge at his work.

Charles Guggenheim: You've been and lived in a number of places. Other writers that you know have lived around and had adventures, been in wars and wrote movies, come back home, and then left. Reynolds never left. Do you know anyone who has stayed in one place as long as he has and still been interesting?
Toni Morrison: Well, there are people who have stayed in one place and become interesting writers, but I'm not so sure they were as interesting as people as he is. But it's a source of great delight to me to know that he has chosen, even before he became ill, to stay in that place, because his is a long-distance mind and that's what's important. It's like saying Emily Dickinson never went anywhere—so what? Or some of the nineteenth-century novelists. Some people really need adventure and odd encounters in order to ignite their imagination, or they need to bump up against some curious anecdote in the newspaper or in a history to ignite their imagination, but Reynolds is an autodidact in that regard. He has always been his own ignition. He always had the seed and the blossom. And knew that the nurturing and the water and the soil was already there. . . .

He's a quintessential American writer. He understands so much about the bravery and the dreams and the failures of men and women who live in these small towns—people who go to big towns and come back or don't go where most of the people in the world live; people who have managed to get through a devastating history in some way that is fascinating and enlightening to read about. I get more of a sense of American people from his work than I do from some of the grander themes in other people's work. He knows the jewelry of them. He knows the intricate clockwork, and he knows not just the sinews but also the way the whole thing works when they make these terrific mistakes or manage certain kinds of reconciliations.

To Be a Black Woman: Review of
Portraits in Fact and Fiction

Review of *Portraits in Fact and Fiction*, edited by Mel Watkins and Jay David. *New York Times Book Review* (23 March 1971): 8. Reprinted by permission of International Creative Management, Inc. Copyright © 1971 by Toni Morrison.

Disassembling a myth—like destroying any refuge—is painful for everybody. Those who have used it are forced to live dangerously, protected loosely and only by skin. Those who have never needed it themselves miss its familiar place in the minds of those who did. Those who would destroy it are frequently trapped in the rubble of their destructions.

High on the list of things-to-be-demythicized is the black woman, and the editors of this anthology propose to dispell "some of the illusions and misconceptions concerning black women." They succeed handsomely in confirming them.

Anthologists do not "write" their books, but they are responsible for them. No less than the authors they choose to reprint, they reveal the fabric of their ideas and the borders of their intelligence. In this collection the fabric is worn and the borders fixed. Although Mel Watkins and Jay David do not specify which "salient or characteristic" aspects they wish to "explicate," there is no confusion about what they are.

With the kindest words, the sweetest euphemisms, the common-est sociological jargon, their *Portraits in Fact and Fiction* manages to re-main fiction. We are left at the end with the same labels provided in the beginning: "laborer," "breadwinner," "sexual myth incarnate— plaything," "protector," "provider," "cushion." In spite of the inclusion of a few splendid pieces, no recognizable human being emerges. What does emerge is an oppressed but sexy, sexy but emasculating, bitch.

The editors bemoan the black woman's sexual exploitation and proceed to include sixteen excerpts remarking it; they suck their teeth over her having been "made the vessel into which white pu-ritanical America poured its repressed sexuality" and sink into a swamp of contradictions to explicate the process. Fascinated by the subject, the editors are nonetheless befuddled by it.

On the one hand "the passive acceptance of any white man" was "part of the black woman's life." On the other—two lines later— "black men . . . were . . . unable to protect their women from sexual assaults by white men." At one point "she accepted the myth [of be-ing the white man's plaything] and often adopted a life-style that actualized it"; at another we read that "the chief concern of most black women has been the black man—whether for his safety or his affection." Still later, ignoring some of their own selections and hundreds of years of evidence to the contrary, they are not embar-rassed to write, "Finally, in the past decade she has become deeply involved in the black man's fight for equal rights." *Finally?* Past *de-cade?* Black *man's* fight?

This book not only supports conflicting myths, it accepts ques-tionable ones. Clucking over "environmental" forces that have forced a masculine role on black women, the editors agree that such a role has emasculated black men, but question none of the widely held myths about black males. It is a curious kind of emasculation which has left the emasculated not just sexually competent, but sexually heroic, and an enviable one if it has bred survivalism, resistance and triumph.

Editorial comment is not the only malignancy of the book. Of the thirty-nine selections, less than a third are by women. The "factual" pieces include the facile generalizations of Calvin C. Herndon, and the racist scholarship of Abram Kardiner and Lionel Ovesey who, along with the editors, speak of families without live-in fathers as "broken." The fiction contains an extremely fraudulent monologue in Langston Hughes's ill-conceived play, *The Mulatto,* and some well-intentioned but slovenly verse by Fenton Johnson and Francis E. W. Harper.

Along with grave error of choosing weak selections, there is a graver one in the uses to which good pieces are put. James Baldwin is used to show the "extreme self-degradation" to which black-white affairs can lead; Maya Angelou's book is picked through to find a section illustrating the "self-doubt" that plagues black women; Richard Wright's recollections are used to reveal her "debasement."

There are, however, some writers whose talent could not, would not, be subverted: Paule Marshall's staggering perception, Don L. Lee's nude eloquence, Jean Toomer's lucidity, W. E. B. Du Bois's intelligence.

Somewhere there is, or will be, an in-depth portrait of the black woman. At the moment, it resides outside the pages of this book. She is somewhere, though, some place, just as she always has been, up to her pelvis in myth, asking those sad, sad questions: When I was brave, was it only because I was masculine? When I was human, was it only because I was passive? When I survived, was it only because my man was dead? And when shiploads of slaves became a race of thirty million, was that really only because I was fecund?

The Family Came First: Review of
Labor of Love, Labor of Sorrow

Review of *Labor of Love, Labor of Sorrow* by Jacqueline Jones. *New York Times Book Review,* (14 April 1985): 11. Reprinted by permission of International Creative Management, Inc. Copyright © 1985 by Toni Morrison.

After slavery, when fresh-born blacks ceased to represent a supply of unpaid labor, agents of the law, the economy, the academy and the Government began to view the black family as problematic in every way. The education of black children, the employment of black adults, housing, medical care, food—whites suddenly began to regard these normal needs as insupportable burdens, and supposed solution to "the problem" of the black family destroyed some families and disfigured others.

That blacks in America were able to maintain families at all and that these families endured after the Civil War is amazing. Perhaps because of this unexpected survival, historians usually treat the black family as a special phenomenon or trivialize it beyond recognition. Not so in *Labor of Love, Labor of Sorrow,* Jacqueline Jones's perceptive, well-written study of black women in the labor force from slavery to the present.

Placing the black family center stage in such a history as this is itself a singular idea, for which we owe the author gratitude. Miss Jones, who teaches history at Wellesley College, has made a valuable contribution to scholarship about black women on several counts.

Labor of Love, Labor of Sorrow exorcises several malignant stereotypes and stubborn myths, it is free of the sexism and racism it describes, and it interprets old data in new ways.

Miss Jones shows how the need to maintain family life shaped the work habits and choices of blacks in general and black women in particular. Examining black women as laborers is one thing; examining this labor force in the context of its life-and-death struggle to save the family is quite another. The attempt to annihilate black families was so spirited that every effort to protect those families was seen as nothing less than sabotage. A male slave who ducked off the plantation to go fishing was perceived as a loafer rather than a provider. Similarly, after slavery, when free black women stayed at home to care for their children (a duty and virtue for white women), they were said to be "doing nothing" and to have "played the lady" by demanding that their husbands "support them in idleness."

Like a silent, underground river, family priorities run through the work choices blacks made after and during slavery. "Freed blacks resisted both the northern work ethic and the southern system of neoslavery," Miss Jones writes. "The full import of their preference for family sharecropping over gang labor becomes apparent when viewed in a national context. The industrial North was increasingly coming to rely on workers who had yielded to employers all authority over their working conditions. In contrast, sharecropping husbands and wives retained a minimal amount of control over their own productive energies and those of their children on both a daily and seasonal basis. Furthermore, the sharecropping system enabled mothers to divide their time between field and housework in a way that reflected a family's needs. The system also removed wives and daughters from the menacing reach of white supervisors. Here were tangible benefits of freedom that could not be reckoned in financial terms."

Though slave women are stereotypically thought of as house servants, 95 percent of them were fieldworkers who had the same workload as men. And contrary to the notion that black women during slavery regarded kitchen work as a "promotion" from fieldwork, most sought the latter to be farther away from white supervision and closer to their own families. Deliberate ineptitude in the kitchen seems to have been the easiest route out of the big house. And this maneuver was echoed in the refusal of black domestics to "live in" when they reached the city.

Of signal importance is that blacks often decided to migrate to urban centers to get better education for their children—a priority equal to (if not greater than) the hope of more and better work. Another manifestation of the priority of the family is that blacks repeatedly chose collectivism based on kinship over "individualistic opportunity." Miss Jones does justice to this seldom recognized characteristic of black people and suggests that this collectivism accounts for the rapid spread of black protest in the 1960s.

Once again the myth of the emasculating black matriarch is deftly punctured here. Miss Jones supplies more evidence (there seems never to be enough to get rid of the myth) showing that during and after slavery black women were not the lone protectors of their families and black men traditionally risked their lives trying to defend their wives and children. The author's refusal to assert female competence at the expense of male roles is refreshing.

Historians usually speak of white women as though they primarily supported black causes. Other than Miss Jones, few writers have mentioned that white women could be as racist as their men. Appropriately, Miss Jones distinguishes the kind of white women who cried "Lynch her!" to black schoolgirls in Little Rock, Arkansas, from those who worked hard on black causes.

Rather than simply looking at data, Miss Jones sees them. In so doing she has turned an arc light on several dark and unexplored corners. There is a marvelous passage on dressing up—how important ribbons, hats, shoes and colorful dresses were to impoverished black women. Films, plays, newspaper cartoons and advertisements once joked about the way black women dressed up, and white women sometimes felt outrage at, and contempt for, black women's choices of fashion. In the mid-1860s, in Wilmington, North Carolina, Miss Jones writes, quoting an observer, white women took "great offense" at black women's wearing veils and gave up the style altogether.

The book contains a surprising analysis of how *Ebony* magazine— a magazine dominated by men at its inception—encouraged black women by closely chronicling their accomplishments. There is a discussion that links the way black women nourished the civil rights movement with the way they protected and encouraged runaway slaves. Feeding runaways with provisions stolen from the mistress's pantry during slavery grew into giving banquets for civil rights activists during the 1960s. Spirituals sung in clandestine slave services became rallying songs at protest meetings.

Though she provides a context for joining the African past to the Afro-American present, Miss Jones is not at all optimistic about the future. She believes that the black women's unprecedented strength can no longer ward off the quite precedented assaults on the black family. But in calling for "a massive public works program [and] a 'solidarity wage' to narrow the gap between the pay scales of lower- and upper-echelon workers," she is exchanging one dependency for another. If Miss Jones is right, if the traditional "make a way out of no way" resourcefulness of black women can't save the black family and blacks are still at the Government's mercy, then they face their gravest danger yet.

Fully half this book is devoted to strategies slaves and newly freed women used to balance labor with family. As well done as it is, this section is the luxury we pay for by having less of Miss Jones's scholarship about events of the 1970s and '80s. The sections of this book that deal with more recent history merely track events without offering insights into them. Perhaps a separate text is needed to tell us exactly how, among modern blacks, the expression "Hey, mama" took on sexual connotations; how marriage came to be perceived as a barrier to self-fulfillment; and how black children came to be viewed as the Typhoid Marys of poverty rather than the victims they in fact are. Such an analysis is outside the scope of this book but not beyond Miss Jones's gifts.

Toni Morrison on a Book She Loves:
Gayl Jones's *Corregidora*

Review of *Corregidora* by Gayl Jones. *Mademoiselle* (May 1975): 14. Reprinted by permission of International Creative Management, Inc. Copyright © 1975 by Toni Morrison.

I wanted to write about some reading experience I had recently . . . something that moved me enormously and that I wanted to talk about to other people. Or to write about something I had read a long time ago that in some way affected my life. In the latter category, there was a good deal to choose from: Kafka was a great education for me, as was Auerbach, as was Camara Laye, as was . . . but it was hopeless. As clearly as I remembered the impact of those works, I had forgotten the excitement, the passion that I must have had. So I thought of recent books I had read, and realized, as all editors do, that while they read all of the time, are burdened with that responsibility night and day, there was very little that I had read that made some deep and abiding impression on me. Having to read so many manuscripts leaves one very little time for reading for pleasure. The reading of manuscripts is very like a constant deluge: two an evening, perhaps, plus the reading of many manuscripts for contests, and prizes for foundations and schools, plus the courtesy reading of friends, plus the critical readings for colleagues. In that whirlpool of print, it is very unlikely that a nerve is hit. The best that happens is that something is brilliantly done and you recognize the brilliance and say so. Seldom have I been sucked into a piece of writing that stirs responses in me other than critical approval. In other words, a reading experience that creates delight, that strips away editorial expertise and goes straight to the jugular. Something that reduces me to a hungry reader and not a professional one. But it did happen . . . once and recently.

A huge box came to me from a friend. The work of a student. There were hundreds and hundreds of pages in this box. So formidable a package could not be tackled lightly or quickly. Every time I looked at it, my heart sank, and I wondered who would be so callous as to send me "all" of the literary output of a student and expect a reasonable response. I kept putting it off. The presence of this box intimidated me and finally it threatened me. If I didn't read it, I would never get rid of that presence.

One Saturday morning I had two hours before I had to take the children somewhere. I went into the bedroom and opened the box. This would be the perfect time to browse through the stuff, get a few ideas about what was wrong with it, and get in touch with my friend with recommendations and guidelines for improvement. I sat on the edge of the bed, tentatively, half leaning, holding the pages in such a way that they could be immediately returned to their box. I never shifted my position, never got comfortable on the bed. Two and a half hours later, the children came banging in wanting to know when I was going to get ready. My leg was asleep under me and I raised my eyes to them in what must have been disbelief. I had been helplessly caught in the work of a twenty-four-year-old girl named Gayl Jones. A short novel she had written called *Corregidora*. What was uppermost in my mind while I read her manuscript was that no novel about any black woman could ever be the same after this. This girl had changed the terms, the definitions of the whole enterprise. So deeply impressed was 1 that I hadn't time to be offended by the fact that she was twenty-four and had no "right" to know so much so well. She had written a story that thought the unthinkable; that talked about the female requirement to "make generations" as an active, even violent political act. She had described the relationship between a black woman and black man as no one else ever had with precision, ruthlessness and wisdom. She had lit up the dark past of slave women with klieg lights and dared to discuss both the repulsion and the fascination of these relationships.

Ursa Corregidora, the last of the line, is legend, phoenix, ghost, sister-love. A kind of combination Billie Holiday and Fannie Lou Hamer. Poignant, frail and knee-buckling. She was every wilted gardenia, and every plate of butterbeans. She was lye cooked in hominy.

I shuddered before the awesome power of this young woman. Even now, almost two years later, I shake my head when I think of her, and the same smile of disbelief I could not hide when I met her, I feel on my mouth still as I write these lines.

Ursa Corregidora is not possible. Neither is Gayl Jones. But they exist.

Going Home with Bitterness and Joy: Review of *South to a Very Old Place* by Albert Murray

Review of *South to a Very Old Place* by Albert Murray. *New York Times Book Review* (2 January 1972): 5. Reprinted by permission of International Creative Management, Inc. Copyright © 1972 by Toni Morrison.

In his latest book, Albert Murray employs a style that allows for the fruitful marriage of instinct and intellect. In *South to a Very Old Place*, he is dealing with an experience that can only be impoverished if one is rejected for the other—the experience of going home. On this journey, Murray proposes to rediscover not just the history of black America, but the meaning of that history—the true meaning of the involvement of blacks and whites in the United States that lies beneath the facts of their surface relationship. Using the resources of the intellect and the emotions, he is able to probe deeper and render that experience as both concept and image.

Murray describes his nonfiction as "an effort to play literary vamps and intellectual riffs equivalent to the musical ones Duke Ellington feeds his orchestra from his piano." His perceptions are firmly based in the blues idiom, and it is black music no less than literary criticism and historical analysis that gives his work its authenticity, its emotional vigor and its tenacious hold on the intellect. His special gift is in the manipulation of politics and poetry, of art and history, of folklore and statistics—a manipulation so deft it is impossible, un-necessary and certainly undesirable to separate them.

Since this is a book about a black man going home to Southland U.S.A., it is a highly political work, focusing on the distinct but in-timate universes of black and white that are America's past, present and future. "After all that instantaneous, popeyed, no-matter-how-fleeting-expression of drawing room outrage you register at the im-propriety of all that . . . blue-eyed [Southern white] talk when you hear it outside the South is perhaps as much an expression of kin-ship as of aginship whether you can admit it or not."

Thus Murray's going home, like the return of any black born in the South, takes on a special dimension. Along with an intimacy with its people and ties to its land, there is a separateness from both the people and the land—since some of the people are white and the land is not really his. This feeling of tender familiarity and brutish alienation provides tension and makes the trip down home delicate in its bitterness and tough in its joy.

But Albert Murray is not simply taking a trip home, he is also creating it; the creation is made up of music, literature, geography, memory and quest. He does have questions, and these questions determine his route. To get back down south he goes first to New Haven to see C. Vann Woodward (as a Southerner he didn't have to go to Oxford to learn about slave categories) seeking a reaction to "up-north cocktail-party glibness about the alleged historical differ-ences and natural antagonisms between the descendents of the so-called field Negroes and house Negroes," Woodward's answer, says Murray, would "stand up very well in all of the barbershops you have ever known."

Of Robert Penn Warren, another Southerner, he asks the origin of the "fugitive" metaphor among the Fugitive Poets. (What could "fugitive" mean to those white Southern poets that it didn't mean to blacks?) In Greensboro, he questions Edwin Yoder on the influence and impact of Uncle Remus-Aunt Hagar relationships on white Southern youth.

"It is European theory-oriented New York intellectuals, not courthouse-square Southerners who are most likely to mistake the concrete virtues of Uncle Remus (and Aunt Hagar) for the abstract attributes of Rousseau's 'noble savage.' To the white Southerner who as a little boy sat at his feet (and went fishing, hunting and on journeys with him) and as a young man served his agricultural and technological apprenticeship under him, Uncle Remus was not only a fundamental symbol of time-honored authority, he was also, as they say in New York, A FATHER FIGURE!, whose sense of complexity and whose intellectual sophistication is anything but that of a 'noble savage.'"

And "in view of all the recent New York drawing-room theories about black matriarchs what is passing strange is that none of the big fatheaded Marx-plus-Freud-oriented experts on black identity who are so glib about family structures and filial relationships otherwise have made absolutely nothing of the fact that white boys from the 'best' Southern families have not only almost always claimed to have had black mammies but have also invariably depicted them as representing the quintessence of Motherhood! Many white Southerners go around talking about white womanhood or really about white girlhood which is to say bellehood, but the conception of *Motherhood,* for some reason almost always comes out *black!*"

Of Jack Nelson (*Los Angeles Times*) and Joe Cummings (*Newsweek,* Atlanta Bureau) he asks why the journalistic view of civil rights is so full of compassion (so easily denigrated to condescension) and so scarce in objectivity that it does not accurately chart revolutionary change?

These various confrontations with Southern whites (liberal, progressive) point up the South-born black's curious relationship to Southern whites: the intimacy and alienation, the "kinship againship." For Robert Penn Warren is not only an author most perceptive about black life in the South, he is also "Red Scarborough in the old Texaco filling station." C. Vann Woodward is "the spitting image of the old Life and Casualty Insurance man" as well as the one historian who "made a special point of saying . . . 'I am prepared to maintain . . . that so far as culture is concerned, all Americans are part-Negro'"—including Afro-Americans who are part Negro too.

Using his own Aunt Hagar–Uncle Remus–trained radar, as well as his enormous gift for understanding what he has read, Murray examines the Southern sensibility of Walker Percy, David L. Cohn, the Hodding Carters, William Faulkner, Thomas Wolfe and a host of others. Always with fresh, when not lucid, insight.

Moving from white South to black South, memory plays a heavier role than investigation. Murray's recollections and rediscoveries about his black Alma Mater are nothing less than obligatory reading. Black colleges are an anomaly in education, looked upon as a problem to be solved or defined. Is the fact of their existence racist? separatist? nationalist? Or is it simply bourgeois "making it"?

Murray's chapter on Atlanta University makes me wonder why a political explanation is needed at all; black colleges clearly educated, stimulated and prepared generations of blacks for the lives they chose or were forced to lead. Never mind the "better" white schools, there is a pride-pure belonging, a supportive identity that black colleges seem to foster.

It is in Mobile, Alabama, however, that Murray's metaphor of Home takes shape. There Murray illustrates the nature and quality of the separateness: what "nigger" means to whites and what it means to blacks; what "boy" means to whites and what its use means to blacks.

"When you heard them saying 'boy' to somebody you always said mister to, you knew exactly what kind of old stuff they were trying to pull. They were trying to pretend that they were not afraid, making believe that they were not always a split second away from screaming for help. When they said Uncle or Auntie they were saying: You are not a nigger because I am not afraid. If you were really a nigger I would be scared to death. They were saying: You are that old now and more careful now so I don't have to be afraid anymore; because now you are a darkey—a good old darkey, so now my voice can be respectful, can remember the authority of reprimands that were mammy-black and the insightfulness that was uncle-black, now I can be respectful not only of age—as of death but also of something else: survival against such odds." Here especially the book is at its best, destroying as it does some fashionable socio-political interpretations of growing up black.

But it is precisely because of his extraordinary perception that it is most surprising to find Murray short-sighted in his concept of the *Afro* part of Afro-Americans. One of the things about which almost all white people seem to agree is the unreconcilable differences among black Americans, black Africans, West Indians, etc. In spite of all evidence to the contrary—including the white man's own invention and definition of race—one has only to hint that the blacks of one continent have a relationship with blacks of another to see hackles rise. With very few exceptions white anthropologists, who will hear nothing denigrating about the whole of Africa do not even trouble to hide their contempt for Afro-Americans.

American scholars who champion black American efforts indiscriminately shy away from any research connecting black American art with Africa; linguists busy with black English spend time describing what American blacks say but never why they say it—the relationship of the language blacks brought to this continent with the language they now speak. The tentative ever so romantic threads black Americans try to spin toward Africa are repeatedly cut, and we hear of shattering culture shocks and rejection from Africans. Obviously a strong identification of black people from all over the world with each other (forced, awkward or sentimental as it may be at first) is as frightening a thought to racism as the gathering of the poor of all nations under one compelling idea is to imperialism.

It is understandable that when white people (accustomed to categorizing and ranking everything) meet an African they raise him one rung above his American brother; even understandable for black people to talk about "barefooted Africans" having nothing in common with themselves. What is puzzling is a black intellectual, all that Harlem rap and jazz-aficionado stuff notwithstanding, of whatever persuasion, who builds dichotomy from diaspora.

Murray questions much in this book, but he does not question those hometown blacks who say: "Every time somebody come up with some of all that old West Indian banana-boat jive about the 'block mon' I tell them, and I been saying it all these years and ain't about to bite my tongue. I tell them, ain't nobody doing nothing nowhere in Africa and nowheres else that this white man right here don't want them to do. I tell them. Every time a goddam African put a dime in a telephone, a nickel of it come right over here to this same white man. . . . All y'all want to go back to Africa, you welcome to go. . . . I'm going to get my college boys trained to go to New York City and Washington, D.C., and get next to something. . . . Them Africans going to take one look . . . and they going to have you writing letters back over here to this same old dog-ass white man in the

United States of America asking for money. Hey, wait. Hey, listen to this. Ain't going to let them get no further than the goddam waterfront."

He goes further in his own reflections: "You also think about how *shared experience* has been a far greater unifying force for so-called black Americans than *race* as such has ever been to the peoples of Africa. It is not the racial factor of blackness as such which is crucial among Africans any more than whiteness as such kept the peace among the peoples of Europe. But all you do is shake your head laughing along with everybody else."

One wishes he had done rather more than shake his head and laugh. It is very difficult to know what to do with that kind of misinformation. In all of his references to the many books he has read, he never once mentions the work of any black writer outside the United States. We assume not that Murray is ignorant of such writers but that he is ignoring them. I don't meant to fret the point and suggest it depreciates the book's value, but on the other hand I mean to do exactly that.

After all, Murray called his book *South to a Very Old Place*. The history of black Americans neither begins nor ends in Mobile, Alabama; its true meaning will stay hidden from any black who does not know that there is another place even South-er and much, much older.

On *The Radiance of the King* by Camara Laye

Review of *The Radiance of the King* by Camara Laye. *New York Review of Books* (9 August 2001): 18+. Also published as introduction to 2001 edition of the novel, published by *NYRB*. Reprinted by permission of International Creative Management, Inc. Copyright © 2001 by Toni Morrison.

1.

Of the velvet-lined offering plates passed down the pews on Sunday, the last one was the smallest and the most nearly empty. Its position and size signaled the dutiful but limited expectations that characterized most everything in the Thirties. The coins, never bills, sprinkled there were mostly from children encouraged to give up their pennies and nickels for the charitable work so necessary for the redemption of Africa. Such a beautiful word, Africa. Unfortunately its seductive sound was riven by the complicated emotions with which the name was associated. Unlike starving China, Africa was both ours and theirs; us and other. A huge needy homeland none of us had seen or cared to see, inhabited by people with whom we maintained a delicate relationship of mutual ignorance and disdain, and with whom we shared a mythology of passive, traumatized otherness cultivated by textbooks, films, cartoons, and the hostile name-calling children learn to love.

World War II was over before I sampled fiction set in Africa. Often brilliant, always fascinating, these narratives elaborated on the very mythology that accompanied those velvet plates floating between the pews. For Joyce Cary, Elspeth Huxley, H. Rider Haggard, Africa was precisely what the missionary collection implied: a dark continent in desperate need of light. The light of Christianity, of civilization, of development. The light of charity switched on by simple human pity. It was an idea of Africa fraught with the assumptions of a complex intimacy coupled with an acknowledgment of profound estrangement. This combination of ownership and strangeness unfettered the imagination of fiction writers and, just as it had historians and explorers, enticed them into projecting a metaphysically void Africa ripe for invention.

Literary Africa—outside, notably, of the work of some white South African writers—was an inexhaustible playground for tourists and foreigners. In the novels and stories of Joseph Conrad, Isak Dinesen, Saul Bellow, Ernest Hemingway, whether imbued with or struggling against conventional Western views of benighted Africa, their protagonists found the continent to be as empty as the collection plate—a vessel waiting for whatever copper and silver imagination was pleased to place there. Accommodatingly mute, conveniently blank, Africa could be made to serve a wide variety of literary and/or ideological requirements: it could stand back as scenery for any exploit, or leap forward and obsess itself with the woes of any foreigner; it could contort itself into frightening malignant shapes in which Westerners could contemplate evil, or it could kneel and accept elementary lessons from its betters.

For those who made either the literal or the imaginative voyage, contact with Africa, its penetration, offered thrilling opportunities to experience life in its inchoate, formative state, the consequence of which experience was knowledge—a wisdom that confirmed the benefits of European proprietorship and, more importantly, enabled a self-revelation free of the responsibility of gathering overly much actual intelligence about African cultures. So big-hearted was this literary Africa, its invitation to explore the inner life was never burdened by an impolite demand for reciprocal generosity. A little geography, lots of climate, a few customs and anecdotes became the canvas upon which a portrait of a wiser or sadder or fully reconciled self could be painted.

In Western novels published up to and throughout the 1950s, Africa, while offering the occasion for knowledge, seemed to keep its own unknowableness intact. Very much like Marlow's "white patch for a boy to dream over." Mapped since his boyhood with "rivers and lakes and names, [it] had ceased to be a blank space of delightful mystery. . . . It had become a place of darkness." What little could be known was enigmatic, repugnant, or hopelessly contradictory. Imaginary Africa was a cornucopia of imponderables that resisted explanation; riddles that defied solution; conflicts that not only did not need to be resolved, but needed to exist if the process of self-discovery was to have the widest range of play.

Thus the literature resounded with the clash of metaphors. As the original locus of the human race, Africa was ancient; yet, being under colonial control, it was also infantile. Thus it became a kind of old fetus always waiting to be born but confounding all midwives. In novel after novel, short story after short story, Africa was simultaneously innocent and corrupting, savage and pure, irrational and wise. It was raw matter out of which the writer was free to forge a template to examine desire and improve character. But what Africa never was was its own subject, as America has been for European writers, or England, France, or Spain for their American counterparts.

Even when Africa was ostensibly a subject, its people were oddly dehumanized in ways both pejorative and admiring. In Isak Dinesen's recollections the stock of similes she draws on most frequently to describe the inhabitants belong to the animal world. "The old dark clear-eyed native of Africa, and the old dark clear-eyed elephant—they are alike." The "hind part of a little old woman . . . is like a picture of an ostrich." Groups of men are "herd[s] of sheep," "old mules." Masai finery is "stags' antlers." And in a moment meant to register the poignant heartache of leaving Africa, Dinesen writes of a woman as follows:

> When we met she stood dead still, barring the path to me, staring at me in the exact manner of a Giraffe in a herd, that you will meet on the open plain, and which lives and feels and thinks in a manner unknowable to us. After a moment she broke out weeping, tears streaming over her face, like a cow that makes water on the plain before you.

In that racially charged context, being introduced in the early Sixties to the novels of Chinua Achebe, the work of Wole Soyinka, Ama Ata Aidoo, and Cyprian Ekwensci, to name a few, was more than a revelation—it was intellectually and aesthetically transforming. But coming upon Camara Laye's *Le Regard du roi* in the English translation known as *The Radiance of the King* was shocking. This extraordinary novel, first published in France in 1954 and in the United States in 1971, accomplished something brand new. The clichéd journey into African darkness either to bring light or to find it is reimagined here. In fresh metaphorical and symbolical language, storybook

Africa, as the site of therapeutic exploits or of sentimental initiations leading toward life's diploma, is reinvented. Employing the idiom of the conqueror, using precisely the terminology of the dominant discourse on Africa, this extraordinary Guinean author plucked at the Western eye to prepare it to meet the "regard," the "look," the "gaze" of an African king.

If one is writing within and about an already "raced" milieu, advocacy and argument are irresistible. Rage against the soul murder embedded in the subject matter runs the risk of forcing the "raced" writer to choose among a limited array of strategies: documenting their seething; conscientiously, studiously avoiding it; struggling to control it; or, as in this instance, manipulating its heat. Animating its dross into a fine art of subversive potency. Like a blacksmith transforming a red-hot lump of iron into a worthy blade, Camara Laye exchanged African "enigma" and darkness for subtlety, for literary ambiguity. Eschewing argument by assertion, he claimed the right to intricacy, to nuance, to insinuation—claims which may have contributed to a persistent interpretation of the novel either as a simple race-inflected allegory or as dream-besotted mysticism.

2.

In his portrait of Africa, Camara Laye not only summoned a sophisticated, wholly African imagistic vocabulary in which to launch a discursive negotiation with the West, he exploited with technical finesse the very images that have served white writers for generations. Clarence, the protagonist, is a white European who has disembarked in an unnamed African country as an adventurer, one gathers. The filthy inn in the village where he is living could be taken word for word from Joyce Cary's *Mister Johnson;* his susceptibility to and obsession with smells read like a play upon Elspeth Huxley's *The Flame Trees of Thika;* his European fixation with the "meaning" of nakedness recalls H. Rider Haggard or Joseph Conrad or virtually all travel writing. Reworking the hobbled idioms of imperialism, colonialism, and racism, Camara Laye allows us the novel experience of both being and watching an anonymous interloper discover not a new version of himself via a country waiting for Western imagination to bring it into view, but an Africa already idea-ed, gazing upon the Other.

It is not made clear what compels Clarence's journey. He is not on a mission, or a game hunt, nor does he claim to be exhausted by the pressures of Western civilization. Yet his desire to penetrate Africa is urgent enough to risk drowning. "Twenty times" the tide has carried his boat toward and away from the shore. Quite deliberately and significantly, Camara Laye spends no time describing Clarence's past or his motives for traveling to Africa. He can forgo with confidence a novelist's obligation to provide background material and rely on the conventions of white-man-in-Africa narratives wherein the reason for the quest is itself a prickly question since it often involves less than innocent impulses. In Saul Bellow's *Henderson the Rain King* one chapter opens, "What made me take this trip to Africa? There is no quick explanation"; and another, "And now a few words about my reasons for going to Africa." The answer, forthrightly, is desire: "I want, I want, I want."

Conrad's characters are driven to Africa by passionate curiosity or else assigned, as it were. One way or another we are to believe they have as little choice to make the trip as the indigenous people have to receive them. Hemingway, even as he experiences the continent (empty except for game and servants) as his private preserve, allows his characters to imply the question and hazard emotional answers.

"Africa was where Harry had been happiest in the good times of his life, so he had come out here to start again." "Africa cleans out your liver," Robert Wilson tells Francis Macomber, "burns fat from the soul." Clarence, too, posits the question repeatedly. "'Why did I want to cross that reef at all costs?' he wondered. 'Could I not have stayed where I was?' But stay where? . . . on the boat? Boats are only transitory dwellings! . . . 'I might have thrown myself overboard,' he thought. But wasn't that exactly what he had done?" "'Can that [life beyond death] be the sort of life I have come here to find?'" Whatever the answer, we never expect what Camara Laye offers: an Africa answering back.

Clarence's immediate circumstance is that he has gambled, lost, and, heavily in debt to his white compatriots, is hiding among the indigenous population in a dirty inn. Already evicted from the colonists' hotel, about to be evicted by the African innkeeper, Clarence's solution to his pennilessness (with the habitual gambler's insouciance) is to be taken into "the service of the king." He has no skills or qualities, but he has one asset that always works, can only work, in third-world countries. He is white, he says, and therefore suited in some ineffable way to be adviser to a king he has never seen, in a country he does not know, among people he neither understands nor wishes to.

His sense of entitlement, however, is muted by timidity and absence of esteem, "having lost the right—the right or the luxury—to be angry." He is prevented by a solid crowd of villagers from speaking to the king, but after a glimpse of him from afar, he is resolute. He meets a pair of mischief-loving teenagers and a cunning beggar who agree to help him out of his difficulty with the innkeeper and the surreal trial for debt that follows. Under their hand-holding guidance he travels south, where the king is expected to appear next.

What begins as a quest for paid employment, for escape from the contempt of his white countrymen and unfair imprisonment in an African jail, could easily have become a novel about another desperate Westerner's attempt to reinvent himself. But Camara Laye's project is different: to investigate cultural perception and the manner in which knowledge arrives. The episodes that Clarence confronts trace and parody the parallel sensibilities of Europe and Africa. Different notions of status, civitas, custom, commerce, and intelligence; of law or of law versus morality—all are engaged here in a nuanced dialogue; in scenes of raucous misunderstandings; in resonant encounters with "mythic" Africa.

Challenging the cliché of Africa as sensual and irrational, Camara Laye uses an "inferno of the senses" as a direct route to rationality. What Clarence sees first as dancers "freely improvis[ing], each without paying any attention to his companions," and doing what he believes are "war dances," a "barbaric spectacle," turns out to be dancers performing an intricate choreography in the shape of a star as they surround the king. Village huts that appear to him originally as monotonous, slipshod hovels he sees later as

> magnificent pottery . . . the walls . . . smooth and sonorous as drums or deep bells, delicately, delightfully varnished and patinated, with the good smell of warm brick. . . . Windows like portholes had been let into the walls, just big enough to frame a face, yet not so big that any passing stranger could cast more than a swift glance into the interior of the hut. . . . Everything was perfectly clean: the roofs were newly thatched, the pottery shone as if it had been freshly polished.

Clarence hears indigenous music as "utterly without meaning"; "queer haphazard noise." In the forest that he finds "absolutely still," "completely empty," his companions hear drums announcing not just their arrival but who, specifically, is arriving. The overpowering, repugnant "odor of warm wool and oil, a herdlike odor," becomes "a subtle combination of flower-perfumes and the exhalations of vegetable molds . . . a sweetish, heady, and disturbing odor . . . all-enveloping rather than repellent . . . caressing . . . alluring," and, one might add, addictive. Once he arrives where the king is expected to appear, he is touched, fondled, and spends his nights steeped in carnal pleasures. The author orchestrates the senses as conduits that make information and intelligence available.

Principally, however, the novel focuses its attention on the authority of the gaze. Sight, blindness, shadows, myopia, astigmatism, delusion are the narrative figurations which lead Clarence and the reader to the novel's dazzling epiphany at the end of his journey, when the king turns to face him. Ignorance and lack of insight are signaled by melting horizons, shifting architecture, torpor. People and events require his and our constant revision. Although it is Clarence's wish for oblivion, to "sleep until the day of deliverance," until he can "catch the king's eye," information is all around him if he chooses to gather it. But Clarence looks away from faces, eyes. His habit of staring at the beggar's Adam's apple rather than his eyes costs him dearly. When, finally, he does look, "he thought he saw in them a dishonest look, a kind of irony, too, and perhaps both of these. . . . Something sly, insidious? . . . Something faintly mocking? How could one tell?" When women appear he sees only their "luxuriant buttocks and breasts." Even the African woman he lives with is "no different from the others":

> Akissi would put her face in the porthole's oval frame, and
> Clarence would be able to recognize it as hers. But as soon as

he saw her whole body, it was as if he could no longer see her face: all he had eyes for were her buttocks and her breasts—the same high, firm buttocks and the same pear-shaped breasts as the other women. . . .

Clarence is enslaved, but he refuses to understand the negotiations for his bondage even though they take place in his presence. In his estimation, the conversations following the beggar's proposal to sell him to service the harem of the Noga, the chief of the village, are merely trivial or simply opaque; all subsequent hints of his services he dismisses as babble. When the "mystery" of his bondage becomes so blatant that perception is inescapable, he greets the perception with unease and lame, truncated questions, without genuine curiosity. Even as he gains rank in the village—now that he is of use—and pointed comments mount, he hides behind his innocence. "Felt all over like a chicken on market-day" by the obese eunuch Samba Baloum, Clarence is merely offended by the familiarity, unaware that a deal has been struck. Because African laughter is senseless to him, he never gets the joke or recognizes double-entendre. Dreams loaded with valuable information he finds "silly." Frequently disguised as a dream, disorientation, or confusion, events and encounters designed to invite perception accumulate as Clarence's Western eye gradually undergoes transformation. "Clarence was now perfectly aware that he had been dreaming; but he could also see now that his dream was true."

What counts as intelligence here is the ability and willingness to see, surmise, understand. Clarence's confusion is deeply confusing to those around him. His refusal to analyze or meditate on any event except the ones that concern his comfort or survival dooms him to servitude. When knowledge finally seeps through, he feels "annihilated" by it. Stripped of the hope of interpreting Africa to Africans

and deprived of the responsibility of translating Africa to Westerners, Clarence provides us with an unprecedented sight: a male European, de-raced and de-cultured, experiencing Africa without resources, authority, or command. Because it is he who is marginal,
ignored, superfluous; he whose name is never uttered until he is
"owned"; he who is without history or representation; he who is
sold and exploited for the benefit of a presiding family, a shrewd en-
trepreneur, a local regime; we observe an African culture being its
own subject, initiating its own commentary.

3.

Clarence does indeed find "the life which lies beyond death," but
not before a reeducation process much like Camara Laye's own cultural education in Paris. Born on the first day of 1928 to an ancient
Malinke family in Guinea, Camara Laye attended a Koranic school,
a government school, and a technical college in Conakry. Awarded a
scholarship at the age of nineteen, he left for France in 1947 to study
automobile engineering. Memories of the solitude, poverty, and me-
nial labor that were his lot in Paris became the genesis of his first
book, the autobiographical *L'Enfant noir* (1953), praised and prized
in France. Deep admiration for French art and culture did not rival
his fervent love of his own.

He entered the political climate of postcolonial Guinea and the
strife-ridden relationship between France and Francophone West Africa with the conviction that "the man of letters should contribute
his writing to the revolution." His proud commitment to this blend
of art and politics, freedom and responsibility, had serious and dam-
aging consequences: imprisonment by Sékou Touré, exile under the
protection of Léopold Senghor in Senegal, and a constantly imperiled

existence. Notwithstanding the usual menu of cultural/educational/government posts offered to writers, the trials of exile, and debilitating bouts of illness, Camara Laye lectured, wrote plays, journalism, and, in 1966, twelve years after the publication of *Le Regard du roi*, completed *Dramouss* (translated as *A Dream of Africa*). *Le Maître de la parole* (*The Guardian of the Word*) appeared in 1978. Full of plans for future projects, Camara Laye succumbed to illness and, in 1980, died at the age of fifty-two.

Camara Laye described *L'Enfant noir*—the story of his rural childhood, his education in Guinea's capital and later in Paris—as "what I am." *Dramouss* continues the "what I am" project, keeping close to the author's own life. In this novel a narrator returns to Guinea, where he finds "a regime of anarchy and dictatorship, a regime of violence" words understood to have provoked Sékou Touré. Camara Laye was never to write as overtly politically again, but *Le Maître de la parole* charts the life of the first emperor of the Kingdom of Mali as told by griots, and can be read as a comment on contemporary African politics.

The autobiographical groove Camara Laye settled into was violently disrupted just once. *Le Regard du roi* is his only true fiction. To grasp the force of his talent as a novelist and to fully appreciate the singularity of his project, it is important to be alert to the cultural snares that entangle critical discourse about Africa. Shreds of the prejudices that menace Clarence cling to much of the novel's appraisal. In its explications, the language of criticism applied to Laye's fiction favors "spontaneous wisdom" rather than strategy; spirit as distinct from the visible, comprehensible world; "mute symbols and cryptic messages" over modern complexity; a naturalistic, universal humanism valued as a "gift to white readers" over craftsmanship. Less attention is given to the book's pregnant dialogue; its delicate, almost clandestine, pacing; its carefully governed structure; to how the author's imagery deflates, alters, and addresses certain foundational European values; to his brilliant exploration of the concept of individual rights, the preeminence of money, and the bewildering obsession with the naked body.

Of the many literary tropes of Africa, three are invidious: Africa as jungle—impenetrable, chaotic, and threatening; Africa as sensual but not on its own rational; and the essence or "heart" of Africa, its ultimate discovery, as, unless mitigated by European influence and education, incomprehensible. *The Radiance of the King* makes these assessments concrete in such a way as to invite (not tell) the reader to reevaluate his or her own store of "knowledge."

It is fascinating to observe Camara Laye's adroit handling of certain elements of this mindscape. *Impenetrable Africa.* Clarence is afraid of the forest, seeing it as a wall, very much like the palace wall that appears to have no entrances, and as unnavigable as the maze of rooms through which he must make his escape. Because his trust in his companions is justifiably limited, he enters the forest with trepidation. What he does not trust at all is his own sight. Although his companions exhibit no confusion, Clarence's fear is stupefying. In spite of noting that the forests are "devoted to wine industry," that the landscape is "cultivated," that the people living there give him a "cordial welcome," Clarence sees only inaccessibility, "common hostility," a vertigo of tunnels, invisible paths barred by thorn hedges. The order and clarity of the landscape are at odds with the menacing jungle in Clarence's head. "Where are the paths?" he cries. "There are paths," the beggar answers. "If you can't see them . . . you've only got your own eyes to blame."

Sensual Africa. Clarence's descent into acquiescent stud is a wry comment on the sensual basking that Europeans found so threatening. He enacts the full horror of what Westerners imagine as "going native," the "unclean and cloying weakness" that imperils masculinity. But Clarence's overt enjoyment of and feminine submission to continuous cohabitation reflect less the "dangers" of sexy Africa than the exposure of his willful blindness to a practical (albeit loathsome) enterprise. The night visits of the harem women (whom Clarence continues to believe against all evidence are one woman) are arranged by the nobu, an impotent old man, for the increase of his family rather than for Clarence's indulgence. The deceit is an achievement made possible by the Africans' quick understanding of this Frenchman's intellectual indolence, his tendency toward self-delusion. As mulatto children crowd the harem, Clarence, the only white in the region, continues to wonder where they came from.

Dark Africa. Although the novel is a revision of the white man's voyage into darkness, I do not see the journey, as some readers do, as a progression from European adult corruption to African child-like purity. Nor do the trials Clarence undergoes seem to imitate an Everyman's pilgrimage through sin and self-loathing necessary in order to effect an ultimate baptism. It appears to me that Clarence's voyage is from the metaphorical darkness of immaturity and degradation. Both of these crippling states precede his entrance into the narrative and are clearly dramatized by the adolescent stupidity with which he handles his affairs and the humiliation he has already suffered at the hands of his European compatriots. Camara Laye's Africa is suffused with light: the watery green light of the forest; the blood-red tints of the houses and soil; the sky's "unbearable . . . azure brilliance"; even the scales of the fish-women he sees glimmer "like robes of dying moonlight."

The king's youth and Clarence's nakedness may encourage the

reading of this novel as culminating with an inner child craving and receiving unearned yet limitless love. But the nakedness Clarence insists upon at the end is neither childish nor erotic. Nor is it "shamelessly immodest." It is stark, absolute—like a truth. "'Because of your very nakedness!' the [king's] look seemed to say." He is accepted, loved, and called into view by the royal gaze because he has arrived at the juncture where truth, knowledge, is possible for him; where the "terrifying void that is within [him] . . . opens to receive [the king]."

This openness, the crumbling of cultural armor and the evaporation of ego, is the beginning of an adult knowledge which is, of course, Clarence's salvation and his bliss. But deep in the heart of Africa's Africa is more than the restorative gaze of the king. There at its core is also equipoise—the radiance of his exquisite articulation: "Did you not know that I was waiting for you?"

Foreword to *The Harlem Book of the Dead*

The Harlem Book of the Dead by James Van Der Zee, Owen Dodson, and Camille Billops. Dobbs Ferry, N.Y.: Morgan and Morgan, 1878. Reprinted by permission of International Creative Management, Inc. Copyright © 1978 by Toni Morrison.

It is fashionable these days to hear among photography lovers the cry, "Oh, those early photographers really knew how to take pictures." Part of the enthusiasm is not critical evaluation but simple nostalgia: a love affair with the past made more loving because the beloved is no longer with us and able to assert itself. Part of it is simple weariness—weariness of contemporary photojournalism that comes pouring into our living rooms via newspapers, magazines, television and film documentaries.

When we look at the work of James Van Der Zee, however, the statement is neither sentimental nor reactionary. His photography is truly rare—*sui generis*. What is so clear in his pictures and so marked in his words is the passion and the vision, not of the camera but of the photographer. The narrative quality, the intimacy, the humanity of his photographs are stunning, and the proof, if any is needed, is in this collection of pictures devoted exclusively to the dead about which one can only say, "How living are his portraits of the dead." So living, so "undead," that the prestigious writer, Owen Dodson, is stirred to poetry in which life trembles in every metaphor.

That this remarkable concert of Black subject, Black poet, Black photographer and Black artist focuses on the dead is significant for it is true what Africans say: "The Ancestor lives as long as there are those who remember." *The Harlem Book of the Dead,* conceived and nurtured by Camille Billops, cherishes that remembrance and enlightens us as only memory can.

Foreword to *Writing Red: An Anthology of American Women Writers, 1930–1940*

Writing Red: An Anthology of American Women Writers, 1930–1940, edited by Charlotte Nekola and Paula Rabinowitz. New York: Feminist Press at CUNY, 1987. ix–x. Reprinted by permission of International Creative Management, Inc. Copyright © 1987 by Toni Morrison.

The embrace of women and politics has always had an uneasy history. From Antigone to Angela Davis, patriarchal reactions to that participation have been to trivialize, to rage, to dismiss, or bury. The possibility that one half of the population should get interested in exercising the power the other half takes for granted, or that a female intelligence is keen enough to analyze and fully engage the political issues of the day is still a startling prospect in some quarters. It conjures up defensive language and frightening images—as though Scylla were in league with Charybdis and the navigation of historical waters had been completely denied all male voyagers. Fortunately, efforts to diminish the perceptiveness with which women have entered the political terrain have not always succeeded. A substantial part of feminist scholarship has chosen to investigate that perception and its consequences.

Even so, it is surprising that the literary histories of a singularly radical period in the United States, the 1930s, have, until now, rested on the work of men. Suffrage, as Paula Rabinowitz tells us, has been assumed to have been followed by a feminist void, until, in the wake of the Civil Rights movement, women again turned their attention toward national and, inevitably, feminist politics. The error of that assumption is revealed in these pages, and is nothing less than re- demption for the hundreds of women writers who "immersed them- selves," as Charlotte Nekola reminds us, "in political struggles far re- moved from personal and domestic realms," and who " . . . added gender as another element of political analysis and explored the com- plex relationships among sex, work, and class."

When women take noncompetitive notice of other women, when their sensitivity to the plight of each other traverses the lines that sepa- rate them—class, race, religion, nationality—extraordinary things can happen: poor women see through the bars rich women are caged in; Black women understand the "privileges" of light skin as destruc- tive to the whole race; mothers recognize the dependence of capi- talist bosses on prolific childbearing; female office workers perceive the oppressive complexities of gender and power at the workplace; middle-class women respond to strikers with compassion and intel- ligence. In these and other kinds of experiences represented in this collection, we see clearly that the "1930s radicalism [that] appears to be a masculine preserve" is in fact peopled with questioning, car- ing, socially committed women writers.

The publication of *Writing Red* is itself testimony to this alert, femi- nist generosity: a pair of women scholars (who are also friends) search and excavate buried or dusty records for the work of other women whose interests in social issues both preceded and affected their own; they are encouraged in this work by other women; they find a publishing haven in a women's press. By making it possible for the women writers of the 1930s to live once more in their political context, Charlotte Nekola and Paula Rabinowitz have widened the circle. (And I am personally pleased about the modest contribution that the Schweitzer Chair at the State University of New York at Albany was able to make.)

In praise of this anthology, perhaps I may be forgiven for misappropriating some lines at the close of Muriel Rukeyser's "Absalom." The poem is about the triumph of a mother who has made the death of her miner son *count.*

> *I come forth by day, I am born a second time,*
> *I force a way through, and I know the gate*
> *I shall journey over the earth among the living.*

In *Writing Red* these long-neglected voices are born a second time, and *count.*

The Fisherwoman: Introduction to
A Kind of Rapture: Photographs

A Kind of Rapture: Photographs by Robert Bergman. New York: Pantheon, 1998. i–iv. Reprinted by permission of International Creative Management, Inc. Copyright © 1998 by Toni Morrison.

I am in this river place—newly mine—walking in the yard when I see a woman sitting on the seawall at the edge of a neighbor's garden. A homemade fishing pole arcs into the water some twenty feet from her hand. A feeling of welcome washes over me. I walk toward her, right up to the fence that separates my place from the neighbor's, and notice with pleasure the clothes she wears: men's shoes, a man's hat, a well-worn colorless sweater over a long black dress. The woman turns her head and greets me with an easy smile and a "How you doing?" She tells me her name (Mother Something) and we talk for some time—fifteen minutes or so—about fish recipes and weather and children. When I ask her if she lives there she answers, No. She lives in a nearby village, but the owner of the house lets her come to this spot any time she wants to fish, and she comes every week, sometimes several days in a row when the perch or catfish are running and even if they aren't because she likes eel, too, and they were always there. She is witty and full of the wisdom that older women always seem to have a lock on. When we part, it is with

an understanding that she will be there the next day or very soon
after and we will visit again. I imagine more conversations with her.
I will invite her into my house for coffee, for tales, for laughter. She
reminds me of someone, something. I imagine a friendship, casual,
effortless, delightful.

She is not there the next day. She is not there the following days
either. And I look for her every morning. The summer passes and
I have not seen her at all. Finally I approach the neighbor to ask
about her and am bewildered to learn that the neighbor does not
know who or what I am talking about. No old woman fished from
her wall—ever—and none had permission to do so. I decide that the
fisherwoman had fibbed about the permission and took advantage of
the neighbor's frequent absences to poach. The fact of the neighbor's
presence is proof that the fisherwoman would not be there. During
the months following, I ask lots of people if they know Mother Something. No one, not even people who have lived in nearby villages for
seventy years, has ever heard of her. It becomes obvious: she has not
moved or died; she has lied to me for some unfathomable reason.

I felt cheated, puzzled, but also amused and wonder off and on
if I have dreamed her. In any case, I tell myself, it was an encounter of no value other than anecdotal. Still. Little by little, annoyance
then bitterness takes the place of my original bewilderment. A certain view from my windows is now devoid of her, reminding me every morning of her deceit and my disappointment. What was she
doing in that neighborhood anyway? She didn't drive, had to walk
four miles if indeed she lived where she said she did. How could she
be missed on the road in that hat, those awful shoes? I try to understand the intensity of my chagrin, and why I am missing a woman I
spoke to for fifteen minutes. I get nowhere except for the stingy explanation that she had come into my space (next to it anyway—at

the property line, at the edge, just at the fence where the most inter-esting things always happen), and had implied promises of female comradery, of opportunities for me to be generous, of protection and protecting. Now she is gone, taking with her my good opinion of myself, which, of course, is unforgivable. And isn't that the kind of thing that strangers do and that we fear they will do? Disturb. Be-tray. Prove they are not like us? That is why it is so hard to know what to do with them. The love that prophets have urged us to offer the stranger is the same love which Jean-Paul Sartre could reveal as the very mendacity of Hell. The signal line of *No Exit*, "L'enfer c'est les autres," raises the possibility that "other people" are responsible for turning a personal world into a public hell.

In the admonition of a prophet and the sly warning of an artist, strangers as well as the beloved are understood to tempt our gaze to slide away or to stake claims. Religious prophets caution against the slide, the looking away; Sartre warns against love as possession.

The resources available to us for benign access to each other, for vaulting the mere blue air that separates us, are few but powerful: language, image, and experience, which may involve both, one, or neither of the first two. Language (saying, listening, reading) can encourage, even mandate, surrender, the breach of distances among us, whether they are continental or on the same pillow, whether they are distances of culture or the distinctions and indistinctions of age or gender, whether they are the consequences of social in-vention or biology. Image increasingly rules the realm of shaping, sometimes becoming, often contaminating, knowledge. Provoking language or eclipsing it, an image can determine not only what we know and feel, but also what we believe is worth knowing about what we feel.

These two godlings, language and image, feed and form experience. My instant embrace of an outrageously dressed fisherwoman was in part because of an image on which my representation of her was based; the image was supported by language—swiftly intimate with the curls and curves I recognized. I immediately sentimentalized and appropriated her. Fantasized her as my personal shaman. I owned her or wanted to (and I suspect she glimpsed it). I had forgotten the power of embedded images and stylish language to seduce, reveal, control. Forgot too their capacity to help us to pursue the human project—which is to remain human and to block the dehumanization of others. If we are lazy the godlings can hinder us in that project; if we are alert they can foster it.

But something unforeseen has entered into this admittedly oversimplified menu of our resources. Far from our original expectations of increased intimacy and broader knowledge, routine media presentations deploy images and language that narrow our view of what humans look like (or ought to look like) and what in fact we are like. Successful merchandising, pivoting as it does on standards and generalizations, limits our scope in order to delimit our desire and in so doing abjure those who do not or cannot buy. While succumbing to the perversions of media can blur vision, resisting them can do the same. I was clearly and aggressively resisting such influences in my encounter with the fisherwoman. Art as well as the market can be complicit in the sequestering of form from formula, of nature from artifice, of humanity from commodity. Art gesturing toward representation has, in some exalted quarters, become literally beneath contempt. The concept of what it is to be human has altered, and the word *truth* so needs quotation marks around it that its absence (its elusiveness) is stronger than its presence.

Why should we want to know a stranger when it is easier to estrange another? Why should we want to close the distance when we can close the gate? Appeals in arts and religion for comity in the Common Wealth are faint.

It took some time for me to understand my unreasonable claims on that fisherwoman. To understand that I was longing for and missing some aspect of myself, and that there are no strangers. There are only versions of ourselves, many of which we have not embraced, most of which we wish to protect ourselves from. For the stranger is not foreign, she is random; not alien but remembered; and it is the randomness of the encounter with our already known—although unacknowledged—selves that summons a ripple of alarm. That makes us reject the figure and the emotions it provokes—especially when these emotions are profound. It is also what makes us want to own, govern, or administrate the Other. To romance her, if we can back into our own mirrors. In either instance (of alarm or false reverence), we deny her personhood, the specific individuality we insist upon for ourselves.

Occasionally there arises an event or a moment that one knows immediately will forever mark a place in the history of artistic endeavor. Robert Bergman's portraits represent such a moment, such an event. In all its burnished majesty his gallery refuses us unearned solace and one by one by one each photograph unveils *us*, asserting a beauty, a kind of rapture, that is as close as can be to a master template of the singularity, the community, the unextinguishable sacredness of the human race.

Politics and Society

On the Backs of Blacks

In *The Debate over the Changing Face of America*, edited by Nicoluas Miller. New York: Touchstone Books, 1994. 97–100. Reprinted by permission of International Creative Management, Inc. Copyright © 1994 by Toni Morrison.

Fresh from Ellis Island, Stavros gets a job, shining shoes at Grand Central Terminal. It is the last scene of Elia Kazan's film *America, America,* the story of a young Greek's fierce determination to immigrate to America. Quickly, but as casually as an afterthought, a young black man, also a shoe shiner, enters and tries to solicit a customer. He is run off the screen—"Get out of here! We're doing business here!"—and silently disappears.

This interloper into Stavros's workplace is crucial in the mix of signs that make up the movie's happy-ending immigrant story: a job, a straw hat, an infectious smile—and a scorned black. It is the act of racial contempt that transforms this charming Greek into an entitled white. Without it, Stavros's future as an American is not at all assured.

This is race talk, the explicit insertion into everyday life of racial signs and symbols that have no meaning other than pressing African Americans to the lowest level of the racial hierarchy. Popular culture, shaped by film, theater, advertising, the press, television, and literature, is heavily engaged in race talk. It participates freely in this most enduring and efficient rite of passage into American culture: negative appraisals of the native-born black population. Only when the lesson of racial estrangement is learned is assimilation complete. Whatever the lived experience of immigrants with African Americans—pleasant, beneficial, or bruising—the rhetorical experience renders blacks as noncitizens, already discredited outlaws.

All immigrants fight for jobs and space, and who is there to fight but those who have both? As in the fishing ground struggle between Texas and Vietnamese shrimpers, they displace what and whom they can. Although U.S. history is awash in labor battles, political fights, and property wars among all religious and ethnic groups, their struggles are persistently framed as struggles between recent arrivals and blacks. In race talk the move into mainstream America always means buying into the notion of American blacks as the real aliens. Whatever the ethnicity or nationality of the immigrant, his nemesis is understood to be African American.

Current attention to immigration has reached levels of panic not seen since the turn of the century. To whip up this panic, modern race talk must be revised downward into obscurity and nonsense if antiblack hostility is to remain the drug of choice, giving headlines their kick. PATTERNS OF IMMIGRATION FOLLOWED BY WHITE FLIGHT, screams the *Star-Ledger* in Newark. The message we are meant to get is that disorderly newcomers are dangerous to stable (white) residents. Stability is white. Disorder is black. Nowhere do we learn what stable middle-class blacks think or do to cope with the "breaking waves of immigration." The overwhelming majority of African Americans, hardworking and stable, are out of the loop, have disappeared except in their less-than-covert function of defining whites as the "true" Americans.

So addictive is this ploy that the fact of blackness has been abandoned for the theory of blackness. It doesn't matter anymore what shade the newcomer's skin is. A hostile posture toward resident blacks must be struck at the Americanizing door before it will open. The public is asked to accept American blacks as the common denominator in each conflict between an immigrant and a job or between a wannabe and status. It hardly matters what complexities, contexts, and misinformation accompany these conflicts. They can all be subsumed as the equation of brand X versus blacks.

But more than a job is at stake in this surrender to whiteness, more even than what the black intellectual W. E. B. Du Bois called the "psychological wage"—the bonus of whiteness. Racist strategies unify. Savvy politicians always include in the opening salvos of their campaigns a quick clarification of their position on race. It is a mistake to think that Bush's Willie Horton or Clinton's Sister Souljah was anything but a candidate's obligatory response to the demands of a contentious electorate unable to understand itself in any terms other than race. Warring interests, nationalities, and classes can be merged with the greatest economy under that racial banner.

Race talk as bonding mechanism is powerfully on display in American literature. When Nick in F. Scott Fitzgerald's *The Great Gatsby* leaves West Egg to dine in fashionable East Egg, his host conducts a kind of class audition into WASP-dom by soliciting Nick's support for the "science" of racism. "If we don't look out the white race will be . . . utterly submerged," he says. "It's all scientific stuff; it's been proved." It makes Nick uneasy, but he does not question or refute his host's convictions.

The best clue to what the country might be like without race as the nail upon which American identity is hung comes from Pap, in Mark Twain's *Huckleberry Finn*, who upon learning a Negro could vote in Ohio, "drawed out. I says I'll never vote ag'in." Without his glowing white mask he is not American; he is Faulkner's character Wash, in *Absalom, Absalom!* who, stripped of the mask and treated like a "nigger," drives a scythe into the heart of the rich white man he has loved and served so completely.

For Pap, for Wash, the possibility that race talk might signify nothing was frightening. Which may be why the harder it is to speak race talk convincingly, the more people seem to need it. As American blacks occupy more and more groups no longer formed along racial lines, the pressure accelerates to figure out what white interests really are. The enlisted military is almost one-quarter black; police forces are blackening in large urban areas. But welfare is nearly two-thirds white; affirmative-action beneficiaries are overwhelmingly white women; dysfunctional white families jam the talk shows and court TV.

The old stereotypes fail to connote, and race talk is forced to invent new, increasingly mindless ones. There is virtually no movement up—for blacks or whites, established classes or arrivistes—that is not accompanied by race talk. Refusing, negotiating, or fulfilling this demand is the real stuff, the organizing principle of becoming an American. Star-spangled. Race-strangled.

The Talk of the Town

New Yorker (5 October 1998): 31–32. Reprinted by permission of International Creative Management, Inc. Copyright © 1998 by Toni Morrison.

This summer, my plan was to do very selective radio listening, read no newspapers or news magazines, and leave my television screen profoundly, mercifully blank. There were books to read, others to finish, a few to read again. It was a lovely summer, and I was pleased with the decision to recuse myself from what had become since January The Only Story Worth Telling. Although I wanted cognitive space for my own pursuits, averting my gaze was not to bury my head. I was eager for information, yet suspicious of the package in which that information would be wrapped. I have been convinced for a long time now that, with a few dazzling exceptions, print and visual media have thrown away their freedom and chosen jail instead—have willingly locked themselves into a ratings-driven, money-based prison of their own making. However comfortable the prison may be, its most overwhelming feature is loss of the public. Not able, therefore, to trust reporters to report instead of gossip among themselves, unable to bear newscasters deflecting, ignoring, trivializing information—orchestrating its minor chords for the highest decibel—I decided to get my news, the old-fashioned way: conversation, public eavesdropping, and word of mouth.

I hoped to avoid the spectacle I was sure would be mounted, fearing that at any minute I might have to witness ex-Presidential friends selling that friendship for the higher salaries of broadcast journalism; anticipating the nausea that might rise when quaking Democrats took firm positions on or over the fence in case the polls changed. I imagined feral Republicans, smelling blood and a shot at the totalitarian power they believe is rightfully theirs; self-congratulatory pundits sifting through "history" for nuggets of dubious relevancy.

I did not relinquish my summer plans, but summer is over now and I have begun to supplement verbal accounts of the running news with tentative perusal of C-SPAN, brief glimpses of anchorfolk, squinting glances at newspapers—trying belatedly to get the story straight. What, I have been wondering, is the story—the one only the public seems to know? And what does it mean?

I wish that the effluvia did add up to a story of adultery. Serious as adultery is, it is not a national catastrophe. Women leaving hotels following trysts with their extramarital lovers tell pollsters they abominate Mr. Clinton's behavior. Relaxed men fresh from massage parlors frown earnestly into the camera at the mere thought of such malfeasance. No one "approves" of adultery, but, unlike fidelity in Plymouth Rock society, late-twentieth-century fidelity, when weighed against the constitutional right to privacy, comes up short. The root of the word, *adulterare*, means "to defile," but at its core is treachery. Cloaked in deception and secrecy, it has earned prominence on lists of moral prohibitions and is understood as more than a sin; in divorce courts it is a crime. People don't get arrested for its commission, but they can suffer its grave consequences.

Still, it is clear that this is not a narrative of adultery or even of its consequences for the families involved. Is there anyone who believes that that was all the investigation had in mind? Adultery is the Independent Counsel's loss leader, the item displayed to lure the customers inside the shop. Nor was it ever a story about seduction—male vamp or female predator (or the other way around). It played that way a little: a worn tale of middle-aged vulnerability and youthful appetite. The Achilles' heel analogy flashed for a bit, but had no staying power, although its ultra meaning that Achilles' heel was given to Achilles, not to a lesser man—lay quietly dormant under the cliché.

At another point, the story seemed to be about high and impeachable crimes like the ones we have had some experience with: the suborning of federal agencies; the exchange of billion-dollar contracts for proof of indiscretion; the extermination of infants in illegal wars mounted and waged for money and power. Until something like those abuses surfaces, the story will have to make do with thinner stuff: alleged perjury and "Lady, your husband is cheating on us." Whatever the media promote and the chorus chants, whatever dapples dinner tables, this is not a mundane story of sex, lies, and videotape. The real story is none of these. Not adultery, or high crimes. Nor is it even the story of a brilliant President naïve enough to believe, along with the rest of the citizenry, that there were lines one's enemies would not cross, lengths to which they would not go—a profound, perhaps irrevocable, error in judgment.

In a quite baffling and frustrating manner, it was not a "story" but a compilation of revelations and commentary which shied away from the meaning of its own material. In spite of myriad "titles" ("The President in Crisis"), what the public has been given is dangerously close to a story of no story at all. One of the problems in locating it is the absence of a coherent sphere of enunciation. There seems to be no appropriate language in which or platform of discourse from which to pursue it. This absence of clear language has imploded into a surfeit of contradictory languages. The parsing and equivocal terminology of law is laced with titillation. Raw comedy is spiked with Cotton Mather homilies. The precision of a coroner's vocabulary mocks passionate debates on morality. Radiant sermons are forced to dance with vile headlines. From deep within this conflagration of tony, occasionally insightful, arch, pompous, mournful, supercilious, generous, salivating verbalism, the single consistent sound to emerge is a howl of revulsion.

But revulsion against what? What is being violated, ruptured, defiled? The bedroom? The Oval Office? The voting booth? The fourth grade? Marriage vows? The flag? Whatever answer is given, underneath the national embarrassment churns a disquiet turned to dread and now anger.

African-American men seemed to understand it right away. Years ago, in the middle of the Whitewater investigation, one heard the first murmurs: white skin notwithstanding, this is our first black President. Blacker than any actual black person who could ever be elected in our children's lifetime. After all, Clinton displays almost every trope of blackness: single-parent household, born poor, working-class, saxophone-playing, McDonald's-and-junkfood-loving boy from Arkansas. And when virtually all the African-American Clinton appointees began, one by one, to disappear, when the President's body, his privacy, his unpoliced sexuality became the focus of the persecution, when he was metaphorically seized and body-searched, who could gainsay these black men who knew whereof they spoke? The message was clear: "No matter how smart you are, how hard you work, how much coin you earn for us, we will put you in your place or put you out of the place you have somehow, albeit with our permission, achieved. You will be fired from your job, sent away in disgrace, and who knows?—maybe sentenced and jailed to boot. In short, unless you do as we say (i.e., assimilate at once), your expletives belong to us."

For a large segment of the population who are not African-Americans or members of other minorities, the elusive story left visible tracks: from target sighted to attack, to criminalization, to lynching, and now in some quarters, to crucifixion. The always and already guilty "perp" is being hunted down not by a prosecutor's obsessive application of law but by a different kind of pursuer, one who makes new laws out of the shards of those he breaks.

Certain freedoms I once imagined as being in a vault somewhere, like ancient jewels kept safe from thieves. No single official or group could break in and remove them, certainly not in public. The image is juvenile, of course, and I have not had recourse to it for the whole of my adult life. Yet it is useful now to explain what I perceive as the real story. For each bootstep the office of the Independent Counsel has taken smashes one of those jewels—a ruby of grand-jury secrecy here, a sapphire of due process there. Such concentrated power may be reminiscent of a solitary Torquemada on a holy mission of lethal inquisition. It may even suggest a fatwa. But neither applies. This is Slaughter-gate. A sustained, bloody, arrogant coup d'état. The Presidency is being stolen from us. And the people know it.

I don't regret my "news-free" summer. Getting at the story in that retrograde fashion has been rewarding. Early this week, a neighbor called to ask if I would march. Where? To Washington, she said. Absolutely, I answered, without even asking what for. "We have to prevent the collapse of our Constitution," she said.

We meet tonight.

The Dead of September 11

Vanity Fair (November 2001). Reprinted by permission of International Creative Management, Inc. Copyright © 2001 by Toni Morrison.

Some have God's words; others have songs of comfort for the bereaved. If I can pluck courage here, I would like to speak directly to the dead—the September dead. Those children of ancestors born in every continent on the planet: Asia, Europe, Africa, the Americas, Australia; born of ancestors who wore kilts, obis, saris, gelees, wide straw hats, yarmulkas, goat-skin, wooden shoes, feathers and cloths to cover their hair. But I would not say a word until I could set aside all I know or believe about nations, war, leaders, the governed and un-governable; all I suspect about armor and entrails. First I would freshen my tongue, abandon sentences crafted to know evil— wanton or studied; explosive or quietly sinister; to stand up before falling down. I would purge my language of hyperbole; of its eagerness to analyze the levels of wickedness; ranking them; calculating their higher or lower status among others of its kind.

Speaking to the broken and the dead is too difficult for a mouth full of blood. Too holy an act for impure thoughts. Because the dead are free, absolute; they cannot be seduced by blitz.

To speak to you, the dead of September, I must not claim false intimacy or summon an overheated heart glazed just in time for a camera. I must be steady and I must be clear, knowing all the time that I have nothing to say—no words stronger than the steel that pressed you into itself; no scripture older or more elegant than the ancient atoms you have become.

And I have nothing to give either—except this gesture, this thread thrown between your humanity and mine: I want to hold you in my arms and as your soul got shot of its box of flesh to understand, as you have done, the wit of eternity: its gift of unhinged release tearing through the darkness of its knell.

For a Heroic Writers Movement

Keynote address, delivered to the American Writers Congress, October 1981. Printed in *Political Affairs* 60.12 (December 1981): 14–17. Reprinted by permission of International Creative Management, Inc. Copyright © 1981 by Toni Morrison.

I thought, some weeks ago, when I was asked to address the American Writers Congress, that I would help issue some clarion call for change: change in the status of writers, change from the low esteem in which the writing community is held, change that would restore to us the primacy that has been snatched from us, forbidden to us or that we have lost through carelessness and inattention. But your presence here in numbers of over 3,000 means that the change is already taking place.

There is fever here, and while we try to diagnose causes and prescribe measures for healing, it is wise to keep in mind that fever is a sign of deeply disturbed life—but life nonetheless. The life of America's community of writers is under attack. I thought it would be difficult to convince large numbers of us that it was so. I need not have worried. The thunder in your response to the call to the Congress proves that we know full well that the picture of "vitality in the arts" that promoters like to talk about is a false picture. As Michael Kuston reported in England about art in America, there is "an alarming instability beneath the dazzle." Behind the headlines of blockbusters, in best-seller columns, gossip columns and the columns of balance sheets, at the edge of the set in the talk shows, underneath the froth of book fairs and right in the middle of the world of books, something is very wrong. Unpublished writers are struck dumb, previously published writers are canceled, financially "successful" writers are harassed (internally and externally) to stay "successful" at all costs. The bigger the claim of brilliance and the more excessive the boasts of printings, the more obvious is the contempt in which we are held. We are toys, things to be played with by little kings who love us while we please, dismiss us when we don't.

Something *is* wrong. The puddle of public funds allocated to writers (always the least amount of all the arts) has been reduced to drops. Government support has been so blasted that it is at the moment a gesture of nickels and dimes so humiliating, so contemptuous of writers, that one is staggered by the sheer gall.

Editors are judged by the profitability of what they acquire, not by the way they edit or the talent they nourish. Major publishers—for whom mere solvency is death—are required to burst with growth or attach themselves to a parent bursting with growth. Otherwise they wither. Small presses that do not starve hang on—hungry, feisty and always in danger of eclipse.

That this notion of the writer as toy—manipulable toy, profitable toy—jeopardizes the literature of the future is abundantly clear. But not only is the literature of the near future endangered; so is the literature of the recent past. This country has had an unsurpassed literary presence in the world for several decades now. But it will be lucky, in the coming decade, if it can hold its own. What emerges as the best literature of the 1980s or even the 1990s may be written elsewhere by other people. Not because of an absence of native genius but because something is very wrong in the writers' community. Writers are less and less central to the idea and subject of literature. Whole schools of criticism have disposessed the writer of any place whatever in the critical value of his work. Ideas, craft, vision, meaning—all of them are just so much baggage in these critical systems. The text itself is a mere point of departure for philology, philosophy, psychiatry, theology and other disciplines.

The political consequences for minority writers, dissident writers and writers committed to social change are devastating. For it means that there is no way to talk about what we mean, because to mean anything is not vogue. Just as to feel anything about what one reads is "sentimental" and also not in vogue. If your works are prohibited from having overt or covert meaning—if our meaning has no meaning—then we have no meaning either.

The literature of the past is endangered not only by brilliant intellectualism but also by glaring anti-intellectualism. Apparently there are still such things as books (already written, already loved) that are so evil they must be burnt like witches at the stake for fear of contaminating other books and other minds. Censorship in new and old disguises is rampant. And contempt gives way to fear. There has been a ritual spasm of book snatching—rivaling that in South Africa for pernicious oppressiveness.

I think it is our sense of that danger to both the future and the past that has brought us here. What is it? Does the danger really come from the monolithic publishers or are they symptoms of some larger malady? It is perhaps the mood of a terrified, defensive, bullying nation no longer sure of what the point is? A nation embarrassed by its own Bill of Rights? Burdened by its own constitutional guarantees and promises of liberty and equal protection under the

Law? A country so hungry for a purely imagined past of innocence and clarity that it is willing to subvert the future and, in fact, to declare that there is none, in order to wallow in illusion? If that were the case, if the country as a whole decided to have no future—then one of its jobs would be to stifle, fetter and dismiss the artists it could not whip into market shape. Because a writer let loose on the world, uncompromised and untamed, would notice what had become of the country, and might say so.

You can not have unmarketable writers roaming around if you have opted for an improved past in exchange for no future. After all, the future is hard, even dangerous, because it may involve change and it may involve loss. And writers would say that too.

We are, some of us, significant individual writers in the cultural life of a group or of an institution, but as writers we are no longer central to the cultural life of this country.

Is that the reason? The mood of the country? The times we live in? Have we given over our power and our primacy to others? Or is there something frail in the nature of our work? Much of what we as writers do and how we do it is shaped by our belief in the sacredness of the individual artist and his freedom. Individualism in its particularly interesting American form may be at the heart of our dilemma. The idea of the individual in the artistic arena has its own ambivalence and contradiction, just as it does in the political arena: governance by many committed to preserving the rights of a few. Ralph Ellison said: "In the beginning was the Word—and its contradiction."

The idea of the artist as a free individual is like a mother who has spawned two descendants who swear they are not related. One is populism and one is elitism. Each claims "individual artistic free-dom" as his true progenitor and believes the other to be alien. Popu-lism, anti-intellectualism, marketplace mentality, commercialism—whatever the word, it rests its case on numbers. How many approved it, bought it. If the numbers are large enough, it must be good.

Elitism rests its case on the conviction that that which is rare is better than that which is plentiful. Elitists do not consider the pos-sibility that that which is rare may simply be scarce (like smallpox), not better. If the numbers are small enough, they believe, it must be good. Both elitists and populists have a wonderful faith in quan-tity as arbiter of the good; the most or the least. Both champion individualism—either the literary Darwinism of the marketplace or the individual uncontaminated by the taste of the masses. The result of this fraticide is muddle, bitterness and the sad defenseless-ness that is rife among us. It is this muddled idea of individualism that (misunderstood, misapplied, romanticized) has given us the much-loved portrait of the struggling artist willingly martyred. The portrait of failure, indifference and rebuff has become so dear to us that we support and enfranchise not the artist but his struggle. We applaud not the artistic triumph but the deprivation that preceded it. God forbid you should do it brilliantly and successfully the first time out. We believe so strongly that knowledge comes from pain that we assume knowledge is pain. I am not convinced. For a true genius, it may be easy.

But pain has become part of what we mean by excellence, by achievement. It's such a loved picture—the alienated, isolated, indi-vidual writer, beleagured but fiercely alone. A loved picture, but a truly lethal one. Because if we buy it completely, it keeps us single, weak, disconnected, vulnerable. Ours is a special kind of work. The solitude we need in order to work can be used against us to play up our view of ourselves as loners. Our work is special also because we cannot display it on our own; we need an establishment to publish and distribute it. And our work is vulnerable because we have no sovereignty in the industry that we nourish—we have no real place in the business of our business.

And as lone individuals we never have. Even as heroic individual writers we will never have it. Publishing is a competitive, profit-making industry committed to competing for more profits. And I suspect we would despise it if it were anything else. It is a system that does what it does best because it has had practice at doing it. It is a system that works when it works—and does not work when it doesn't. And it is important to remember that it works the way it does because it is permitted to.

We live in an age of advanced capitalism, disintegrating into banditry. And being published in that atmosphere is debilitating. It tempts us into games devised by other people for more other people, into definitions of our work culled by other people; into professional and personal antagonisms that benefit other people; into knee-jerk vindictiveness; into vanity without pride; into celebrity without status; into a quisling acceptance of the "given-ness" of the marketplace.

Romanticized and misapplied, individualism keeps us self-indulgent. It keeps us ignorant of contracts, of money, of benefits, of rights, of how the partnership between author and publisher ought to work, of the areas that threaten both publisher and writer. It keeps us in an adversary relationship at certain junctures where such a relationship is counterproductive. Individualism can also keep us dependent on foundation largesse, grants, fellowships, campuses, cloisters and handouts. And if things go on in this manner, individualism will idle us—it will keep us from the work we have chosen to do. The political philosophy of the country chants its love of individualism, the nature of our work makes us prize it, and the corporate compulsion of the industry fosters it.

But it is not as individuals that we are abused and silenced; it is as writers. When the gates close, the keeper will not ask whether we wrote for private gratification or public service. He will simply slam down the bar. When books are plucked from shelves or thrown into bonfires be quite clear on one point: the flames will destroy criticism and fiction, poems and history, the eclectic and popular. And the work of a writer who took a lifetime to do one perfect poem will burn just as fast as that of a hugely successful Gothic novelist. When libel suits are filed, the evidence will not turn on whether we were funded by public or private funds or whether our families lent us a tide-me-over.

We may be dreamers or scholars, we may need tranquility or chaos—we may write for posterity or for the hour that is upon us. But we are all workers in the most blessed and mundane sense of that word. And as workers we need protection in the form of data. Who are we? And how many? What do we earn? What is earned of us? What are we entitled to?

We need protection in the form of structure: an accessible organization that is truly representative of the diverse interests of all writers. An organization committed to the rights of the few. And we need protection in the form of clarity, a knowledge of the limits of individualism and the private, indulgent suffering it fosters. We have to stop loving our horror stories. Joyce's *Ulysses* was rejected fourteen times. I don't like that story. I hate it. Fitzgerald burned out and could not work. Hemingway despaired and could not work. A went mad, B died in penury, C drank herself to death, D was blacklisted, E committed suicide. I hate those stories. Great works are written in prisons and holding camps. So are stupid books. The misery does not validate the work. It outrages the sensibility and violates the work. All that those stories mean is that solitude, competitiveness and grief are the inevitable lot of a writer only when there is no organization or network to which he can turn.

We need what I believe we have; 3,000 writers gathered together. To insure freedom of expression we need collective power. If we achieve it, it means our destiny will not leap or languish at the whim of public taste, academic fiat or paraded ignorance. We are already at the barricades. Perhaps that is because what we do is not entirely secular. The emotion that print can produce, the association of the word with superhuman power, drags us to the barricades whether we wish it or not. Anyone writing a primer on oppression would identify writers first and early as those to be watched. And they would be right. Language is holy. To destroy a culture you first denigrate its language. You prohibit its spoken use and limit its printed form. You screen it and filter it until it accommodates itself to the presiding language, the one that has the biggest navy, and the most guns. To control future generations, you must control the word and the books that contain it.

We don't need any more writers as solitary heroes. We need a heroic writers' movement—assertive, militant, pugnacious. That is our mission and our risk: we have chosen it. It is also our power: we have earned it. If just one resolution comes from this Congress, let it be that we remain at the barricades where we belong. We must be more than central. We must be sovereign.

Remarks Given at the Howard University Charter Day Convocation

Howard University, 2 March 1995. Transcribed from a tape recording of the remarks by the *Journal of Blacks in Higher Education* with editorial assistance by Howard University Office of the University Communications. Printed in *Nation* (29 May 1995): 760. Reprinted by permission of International Creative Management, Inc. Copyright © 1995 by Toni Morrison.

Thank you, thank you very much for that very warm and very sustained welcome. Thank you madam president and Mr. Chairman for your kind words and the generosity you have shown to me. This is a very distinct pleasure for me. To come back to the place that has meant a great deal to me. To the place that was formative in ways that were social as well as intellectual. I made lifelong friends here. And I felt always privileged in my encounter with faculty here who really knew how to develop a very fledgling mind.

Howard University both as an institution and as a population has had an extraordinary journey. It entered the world in an interventionist mode and has continued throughout its history to engage with, debate and respond to the most salient, the most passionately held, and the most urgent issues of this nation.

It countered with a vengeance the prevailing nineteenth-century notion that education was not part of the future of African Americans. The prevailing nineteenth-century notion that if by some odd chance higher education were to become available on a large scale, that it would be of no use to have it because the higher plateaus of achievement and influence were closed. Evidence to the contrary is overwhelming and the nation owes Howard University a great deal in terms of the countering of that nineteenth-century notion.

Howard struggled with distress, with shortages, with slashes and long periods as well as intermittent periods of national indifference. Yet, among its alumni are men and women who raised the standards of morality, responsibility and intellect all over the world. Howard negotiated and debated conflicting views on solutions to highly complex, extremely volatile social problems and regarded that debate as its duty. Howard has been much praised. It has also been much maligned and has suffered a step back, even a setback. But it has never suffered defeat. And here it is bigger and in many ways better than it was—128 years old, facing the twenty-first century with the vigor and vision we have come to take for granted. We've come to expect that vigor, that vision because in addition to Howard's obvious triumphs it has also to its credit tough scar tissue, nerves of steel, that walk-on-water determination that characterized its founders and our ancestors and was made testimony in the president's remarks this afternoon.

Its bruises are testimonies accumulated through decades of battling nefarious forces. Forces which we were led to believe despised our existence as a people. And Howard managed to keep a straight face and listened to segregationist rhetoric. Perhaps, because it knew that for three hundred years black people lived in segregationists' houses, were all up in their food [laughter], in the intimate lives of their family and understood that our presence was not repellent but in fact sought after as long as they could control us. I don't know a leading racist who has not written of the perfect relationship he or she had with a loving black adult or child.

So, members of the Howard community went right on disassembling these arguments and positions in order to become the leader in the early civil rights movement, and I am proud to have benefitted from that tradition of argument—argument in the finest sense of the word. Not to destroy an opponent but to discover truth. Of managing the tradition. Of managing dangerously limited resources. Of cherishing excellence. Of nurturing progeny. Of reconfiguration. Of invention. Of creative problem solving that are the signs of modernity. These things all I learned here and have informed that part of me of which I still approve.

I hope you will understand and forgive me for indexing here not the sweetness and the beauty and the conviviality in my recollections of Howard. They are many and at least one is seminal because it was here that I began, when I was an instructor on the faculty, to write the first book I ever published. So I have profoundly pleasant and exciting memories of this place. But I am listing the more sinewy of these impressions because they are the ones that represent aspects of knowledge and features of resilience very much in demand right now.

The vocabulary of our current dispossession has changed. But, its desirability in certain quarters has not changed. And all of these strengths that I mentioned earlier distributed among Howard alumni and among its students—all of these strengths have to be called upon now because they are urgently needed in 1995. Let me be clear in a little scenario that I want to paint that is not contrary to my mode, fiction.

Before there was a final solution, there was a first one. And after the first, there was a second. And after the second, there was a third. Who knows how many more because the descent into a final solution is not a jump, it's one step, and then another, and then another. Sort of like this:

One, construct an interior enemy and use that enemy as both focus and diversion.

Two, unleash and protect the utterance of overt and coded name calling, verbal abuse, and use this *ad hominem* attack as legitimate charges.

Three, enlist, persuade and create sources of information and distributors of information willing to reinforce the enemy's status as an enemy. And the reasons for this willingness are: It is profitable to do so. It grants power to do so. And it works.

Four, reward mindlessness and apathy with little pleasures, tiny seductions—a few minutes on television, a few lines in the press, little pseudo-successes, the illusion of power and influence, a little style, a little consequence.

Five, attack and subvert all representatives or sympathizers with this constructed enemy who have risen to serious power. Unless, of course, the next one is part of their CV because one has to gather from among the enemy collaborators who agree with and sanitize the process of dispossession.

Then, you are able to completely take the next step—pathologize the enemy. For example, recycle scientific racism and the myth of racial superiority in order to neutralize the pathology.

Then, criminalize the enemy, and having criminalized the enemy you can then prepare, budget for, and rationalize the building of holding arenas for the enemy, especially the males and absolutely the children.

Last, maintain at all costs silence.

Forces interested in these solutions to national problems are not to be found in one political party or another. Or one or another wave of a single political party. Democrats have no unsullied history of egalitarianism. Nor are liberals free of agendas for domination. Republicans have housed abolitionists and white supremacists. Conservative, moderate, liberal, right, left, far left, far right, religious, secular, socialist—we must not be blindsided by these Pepsi Cola, Coke-Cola labels because the genius of racism and its succubus twin fascism—that genius is that any political structure can host that virus and virtually any developed country can become a suitable home.

Fascism only talks ideology but it really is just marketing, marketing for power. It's recognizable by its need to purge, the strategies it uses to purge and its terror of truly democratic goals. It changes citizens into taxpayers so individuals become rife with anger at the notion of the public good. It changes citizens into consumers so the measure of our value as humans is not our humanity, nor our compassion, nor our generosity, none of the virtues that human beings aspire to claim. None of that but what we own. And in so doing produces the perfect capitalist. The one who is willing to kill a human being for a product—a sneaker, a jacket, a car, a company. That is the ideal situation for a consumer, lay capitalist society. You don't have to advertise any more. It changes parenting into panicking so that we vote against the education, against the health care, against the safety from weapons, against the interest of our own children.

In 1995, it may wear a new dress, it may buy a new pair of boots, but fascism is not new. The mission of Howard has withstood inclement political weather, many, many, many times, and it will again have to be perhaps a forerunner. For universities all over the country will have ever greater difficulty, greater difficulty than they already have had of preserving freedoms that have already been won but are now threatened. Universities will have to convince themselves that it is still necessary to educate for critical intellects rather than the receptacles of predigested knowledge.

Howard may have to lead other universities into maintaining standards with garrotted resources and the sort of national contempt for complicated reflective thought. I'm convinced it would have to rely ever more strongly on its own historical wealth—the index I recited earlier—every discipline, every department, every program. The natural sciences—in an age when we are still once again defending or explaining the absence of a defense for racial and genetic inferiority. The humanities—while we witness the degradation of scholarship, our scholarship and our artists. Law, the social sciences—all have to be involved as it has always been at this university in that debate. This is life and death.

I have to tell you, nothing is more important than this generation. It is very difficult not to be enormously moved as I sat there listening to the forty-first generation of Howard University choirs since I left. It's important to know nothing, nothing, not us, nothing is more important than our children. And if our children don't think they are important to us, if they don't think they are important to themselves, if they don't think they are important to the world, it's because we have not told them. We have not told them that they are our immortality. We have not told them that they are responsible for producing and leading generations after them. We have not told them the things Howard University told me. For which I will always be grateful. I congratulate you on your steadfastness, on the 128 years and I resummon you to the heights—in fact already cleared—in our past.

Thank you.

The Future of Time: Literature and Diminished Expectations

The 25th Jefferson Lecture in the Humanities, 25 March 1996. Reprinted by permission of International Creative Management, Inc. Copyright © 1996 by Toni Morrison.

Time, it seems, has no future. That is, time no longer seems to be an endless stream through which the human species moves with confidence in its own increasing consequence and value. It certainly seems not to have a future that equals the length or breadth or sweep or even the fascination of its past. Infinity is now, apparently, the domain of the past. In spite of frenzied anticipation of immanent entry into the next millennium, the quality of human habitation within its full span occupies very little space in public exchange. Twenty or forty years into the twenty-first century appears to be all there is of the "real time" available to our imagination. Time is, of course, a human concept, yet in the late twentieth century (unlike in earlier ones) it seems to have no future that can accommodate the species that organizes, employs and meditates on it. The course of time seems to be narrowing to a vanishing point beyond which humanity neither exists nor wants to. It is singular, this diminished, already withered desire for a future. Although random outbreaks of armageddonism and a persistent trace of apocalyptic yearnings have disrupted a history that was believed to be a trajectory, it is the past that has been getting longer and longer. From an earth thought in the seventeenth century to have begun around 4,000 B.C.; to an eighteenth century notion of an earth 168,000 years old; to a "limitless" earthly past by the nineteenth century to Darwin's speculation that one area of land was 300 million years old we see no reason not to accept Bergson's image of a "past which gnaws into the future and which swells as it advances."

Oddly enough it is in the modern West—where advance, progress and change have been signatory features—where confidence in an enduring future is at its slightest.

Pharaohs packed their tombs for time without end. The faithful were once content to spend a century perfecting a cathedral. But now, at least since 1945, the comfortable assurance of a "World without End" is subject to debate and, as we approach year 2000, there is clearly no year 4000 or 5000 or 20,000 that hovers in or near our consciousness.

What is infinite, it appears, what is always imaginable, always subject to analysis, adventure and creation is past time. Even our definitions of the period we are living in have prefixes pointing backwards: post-modern, post structuralist, post colonial, post Cold War. Our contemporary prophecies look back, behind themselves, post, after, what has gone on before. It is true, of course, that all knowledge requires a grasp of its precedents. Still it is remarkable how often imaginative forays into the far and distant future have been solely and simply opportunities to re-imagine or alter the present *as past.* And this looking back, though enabled by technology's future, offers no solace whatsoever for humanity's future. Surrounding the platform from which the backward glance is cast is a dire repulsive landscape.

Perhaps it is the disruptive intervention of telecommunication technology, which so alters our sense of time, that encourages a long-ing for days gone by when the tempo was less discontinuous, closer to our own heartbeat. When time was anything but money. Perhaps centuries of imperialist appropriations of the future of other coun-tries and continents have exhausted faith in our own. Perhaps the visions of the future that H.G. Wells saw—a stagnant body of never rippled water—have overwhelmed us and precipitated a flight into an eternity that has already taken place.

There are good reasons for this rush into the past and the happi-ness its exploration, its revision, its deconstruction affords. One rea-son has to do with the secularization of culture. Where there will be no Messiah, where afterlife is understood to be medically absurd, where the concept of an "indestructible soul" is not only unbeliev-able but increasingly unintelligible in intellectual and literate realms, where passionate, deeply held religious belief is associated with ig-norance at best, violent intolerance at its worst, in times as suspi-cious of eternal life as these are, when "life in history supplants life in eternity," the eye, in the absence of resurrected or reincarnated life, becomes trained on the biological span of a single human being. Without "eternal life," which casts humans in all time to come—forever—the future becomes discoverable space, outer space, which is, in fact, the discovery of more past time. The discovery of billions of years gone by. Billions of years—ago. And it is *Ago* that unravels before us like a skein the origins of which remain unfathomable.

Another reason for this preference for an unlimited past is cer-tainly fifty years of life in the nuclear age in which the end of time (that is human habitation within it) was and may still be a very real prospect. There seemed no point in imagining the future of a spe-cies there was little reason to believe would survive. Thus an obses-sion for time already spent became more than attractive; it became psychologically necessary. And the terrible futureless-ness that accompanied the cold war has not altered so much (in the wake of various disarmaments and freezes and non-proliferation treaties) as gone underground. We are tentative about articulating a long earthly future; we are cautioned against the luxury of its meditation as a harmful deferral and displacement of contemporary issues. Fearful, perhaps, of being likened to missionaries who were accused of diverting their converts' attention from poverty during life to rewards following death, we accept a severely diminished future.

I don't want to give the impression that all current discourse is unrelievedly oriented to the past and indifferent to the future. The social and natural sciences are full of promises and warnings that will affect us over very long stretches of future time. Scientific applications are poised to erase hunger, annihilate pain, extend individual life spans by producing illness-resistant people and disease-resistant plants. Communication technology is already making sure that virtually everyone on earth can "interact" with each other and be entertained, maybe even educated, while doing so. We are warned about global changes in terrain and weather that can alter radically human environment; we are warned of the consequences of maldistributed resources on human survival and warned of the impact of over-distributed humans on natural resources. We invest heavily in these promises and sometimes act intelligently and compassionately on the warnings. But the promises trouble us with ethical dilemmas and a horror of playing God blindly, while the warnings have left us less and less sure of how and which and why. The prophecies that win our attention are those with bank accounts large enough or photo ops sensational enough to force the debates and outline corrective action, so we can decide which war or political debacle or environmental crisis is intolerable enough; which disease, which natural disaster, which institution, which plant, which animal, bird or fish needs our attention most. These are obviously serious concerns. What is noteworthy among the promises and warnings is that other than products and a little bit more personal time in the form of improved health, and more resources in the form of leisure and money, to consume these products and services, the future has nothing to recommend itself.

What will we think during these longer, healthier lives? How efficient we were in deciding whose genes were chosen to benefit from these "advances" and whose were deemed unworthy? No wonder the next twenty or forty years is all anyone wants to contemplate. To weigh the future of future thoughts requires some powerfully visionary thinking about how the life of the mind can operate in a moral context increasingly dangerous to its health. It will require thinking about the generations to come as life forms at least as important as cathedral-like forests and glistening seals. It will require thinking about generations to come as more than a century or so of one's own family line, group stability, gender, sex, race, religion. Thinking about how might we respond if certain our own line would last 2,000, 12,000 more earthly years. It will require thinking about the quality of human life, not just its length. The quality of intelligent life, not just its strategizing abilities. The obligations of moral life, not just its ad hoc capacity for pity.

It is abundantly clear that in the political realm the future is already catastrophe. Political discourse enunciates the future it references as something we can leave to or assure "our" children or—in a giant leap of faith—"our" grandchildren. It is the pronoun, I suggest, that ought to trouble us. We are not being asked to rally for *the* children, but for *ours*. *Our* children stretches our concern for two or five generations. *The* children gestures towards time to come of greater, broader, brighter, possibilities—precisely what politics veils from view. Instead political language is dominated by glorifications of some past decade, summoning strength from the pasted-on glamour of the twenties—a decade rife with war and the mutilation of third world countries; from attaching simplicity and rural calm to the thirties—a decade of economic depression, worldwide strikes and want so universal it hardly bears coherent thought; from the righteous forties when the "good war" was won and millions upon millions of innocent died wondering, perhaps what that word, good, could possibly mean. The fifties, the current favorite, has acquired a gloss of voluntary orderliness, of ethnic harmony, although it was a decade of outrageous political and ethnic persecution. And here one realizes that the dexterity of political language is stunning, stunning and shameless. It enshrines the fifties as a model decade peopled by model patriots while at the same time abandoning the patriots who lived through them to reduced, inferior or expensive healthcare; to gutted pensions; to choosing suicide or homelessness.

What will we think during these longer healthier lives? How successful we were in convincing our children that it doesn't matter that their comfort was wrested and withheld from other children? How adept we were in getting the elderly to agree to indignity and poverty as their reward for good citizenship?

In the realm of cultural analyses not only is there no notion of an extended future, history itself is over. Modern versions of Oswald Spengler's *Decline of the West* are erupting all over the land. Minus, however, his conviction that the modern world contained an unsurpassable "will to the Future." The "landslide" began in 1973 according to Eric Hobsbawn. And that post-sixties date is more or less the agreed upon marker for the beginning of the end. Killing the sixties, turning that decade into an aberration, an exotic malady ripe with excess, drugs and disobedience is designed to bury its central features—emancipation, generosity, acute political awareness and a sense of shared and mutually responsible society. We are being persuaded that all current problems are the fault of the sixties. Thus contemporary American culture is marketed as being in such disrepair it needs all our energy to maintain its feeble life support system.

Seen through the selectively sifted grains of past time, the future thins out, is dumbed down, limited to the duration of a thirty-year Treasury bond. So we turn inward, clutching at a primer book dream of family, strong, ideal, protective. Small but blessed by law, and shored up by nineteenth-century "great expectations." We turn to sorcery: summoning up a brew of aliens, pseudo enemies, demons, false "causes" that deflect and soothe anxieties about gates through which barbarians saunter; anxieties about language falling into the mouths of others. About authority shifting into the hands of strangers. Civilization is neutral, then grinding to a pitiful, impotent halt. The loudest voices are urging those already living in dread of the future to speak of culture in military terms—as a cause for and expression of war. We are being asked to reduce the creativity and complexity of our ordinary lives to cultural slaughter; we are being bullied into understanding the vital exchange of passionately held views as a collapse of intelligence and civility; we are being asked to regard public education with hysteria and dismantle rather than protect it; we are being seduced into accepting truncated, short term, CEO versions of our wholly human future. Our everyday lives may be laced with tragedy, glazed with frustration and want, but they are also capable of fierce resistance to the dehumanization and trivialization that politico-cultural punditry and profit-driven media depend upon.

We are worried, for example, into catalepsy or mania by violence—our own and our neighbors' disposition toward it. Whether that worry is exacerbated by violent images designed to entertain, or by scapegoating analyses of its presence, or by the fatal smile of a telegenic preacher, or by weapons manufacturers disguised as occupants of innocent duck blinds or bucolic hunting lodges, we are nevertheless becoming as imprisoned as the felons who feed the booming prison industry by the proliferation of a perfect product: guns. I say perfect because from the point of view of the weapons industry the marketing is for protection, virility, but the product's real value, whether it is a single bullet, a thousand tons of dynamite or a fleet of missiles, is that it annihilates itself immediately and creates, thereby, the instant need for more. That it also annihilates life is actually a by-product.

What will we think during these longer more comfortable lives? How we allowed resignation and testosteronic rationales to purloin the future and sentence us to the dead end that endorsed, glamorized, legitimated, commodified violence leads to? How we took our cue to solving social inequities from computer games? winning points or votes for how many of the vulnerable and unlucky we eliminated? winning seats in government riding on the blood lust of capital punishment? winning funding and attention by re-vamping 1910 sociology to credit "innate" violence and so make imprisonment possible at birth? No wonder our imagination stumbles beyond 2030—when we may be regarded as monsters to the generations that follow us.

If scientific language is about a longer individual life in exchange for an ethical one; if political agenda is the xenophobic protection of a few families against the catastrophic others; if religious language is discredited as contempt for the non-religious; if secular language bridles in fear of the sacred; if market language is merely an excuse for inciting greed; if the future of knowledge is simply "upgrade," where also might we look for hope in time's own future?

I am not interested here in signs of progress, an idea whose time has come and gone—gone with the blasted future of the monolithic Communist state; gone also with the fallen mask of capitalism as free, unlimited and progressive; gone with the deliberate pauperization of peoples that capitalism requires; gone also with the credibility of phallocentric "nationalisms." But gone already by the time Germany fired its first deathchamber. Already gone by the time South Africa legalized Apartheid and gunned down children in dust too thin to absorb their blood. Gone, gone in the histories of so many nations mapping their geography with lines drawn through their neighbors' mass graves; fertilizing their lawns and meadows with the nutrients of their citizens' skeletons; supporting their architecture on the spines of women and children. No, it isn't progress that interests me. I am interested in the future of time.

Because art is temporal and because of my own interests, my glance turns easily to literature in general and narrative fiction in particular. I know that literature no longer holds a key place among valued systems of knowledge; that it has been shoved to the edge of social debate; is of minimal or purely cosmetic use in scientific, economic discourse. But it is precisely there, at the heart of that form, where the serious ethical debates and probings are being conducted. What does narrative tell about this crisis in diminished expectations?

I could look for an Edith Wharton shouting "Take your life"— that is take *on* your life! For a Henry James (in *A Sense of the Past*) appalled by an ancient castle that encloses and devours its owner. For a William Faulkner envisioning a post-nuclear human voice however puny. For a Ralph Ellison posing a question in the present tense signaling a sly and smiling promise of a newly sighted [visible] future. For a James Baldwin's intense honesty coupled with an abiding faith that the price of the ticket had been paid in full and the ride begun. Those voices have been followed, perhaps supplanted, by another kind of response to our human condition. Modern searches into the past have produced extraordinary conceptual and structural innovations.

The excitement of anticipating a future, once a fairly consistent preoccupation of nineteenth- and early twentieth-century literature, has recently been reproduced in an amazing book by Umberto Eco—*The Island of the Day Before*. And its title makes my point. The genius of the novel's narrative structure is having the protagonist located in the seventeenth century in order to mesmerize us with future possibilities. We are made to take desperate pleasure in learning what we already know to have taken place long ago. And this extraordinary novel is, as the author tells us, "a palimpsest of a rediscovered manuscript." Through its construction and its reading we move forward into an already documented history. When the power and brilliance of many late twentieth-century writers focus on our condition, they often find a rehearsal of the past to yield the most insightful examination of the present and the images they leave with us are instructive.

Peter Hoeg, whose first novel nailed us relentlessly in the present, turns in *History of Danish Dreams* to a kind of time travel (associated with though not similar to Eco's) in which regression becomes progression.

". . . if I persist," Hoeg writes at the end of this novel, "in writing the history of my family, then it is out of necessity. Those laws and regulations and systems and patterns that my family and every other family in Denmark has violated and conformed to and nudged and writhed under for two hundred years are now in fact in a state of foaming dissolution. . . . Ahead lies the future, which I refuse to view as Carl Laurids did: down a gun barrel; or as Anna did: through a magnifying glass. I want to meet it face-to-face, and yet I am certain that if nothing is done, then there will be no future to face up to since although most things in life are uncertain, the impending disaster and decline look like a safe bet. Which is why I feel like calling for help— . . . and so I have called out to the past.

". . . now and again the thought strikes me that perhaps I have never really seen other people's expectations; that I have only ever seen my own, and the loneliest thought in the world is the thought that what we have glimpsed is nothing other than ourselves. But now it is too late to think like that and something must be done, and before we can do anything we will have to form a picture of the twentieth century."

Forming a picture of the twentieth century then—not the twenty-first—is, in this novel, the future's project.

William Gass, in a masterful work, *The Tunnel*, sustains a brilliant meditation on the recent past forever marked by Nazi Germany. In it his narrator/protagonist having completed a "safe" morally ambivalent history of German fascism, a work titled *Guilt and Innocence in Nazi Germany*, finds himself unable to write the book's preface. The paralysis is so long and so inflexible, he turns to the exploration of his own past life and its complicitous relationship to the historical subject of his scholarship—"a fascism of the heart." Gass ends the novel in heartbreaking images of loss,

". . . suppose," he writes, "that instead of bringing forth flowers the bulb retreated to some former time just before it burgeoned, that pollen blew back into the breeze which bore it toward its pistil, suppose the tables were turned on death, it was bullied to begin things, and bear its children backward, so that the first breath didn't swell the lung but stepped on it instead, as with a heavy foot upon a pedal; that there was . . . a rebellion in the ranks, and life picked the past to be in rather than another round of empty clicks called present time. . . . I made . . . a try. I abandoned Poetry for History in my Youth.

"What a journey, though, to crawl in earth first, then in filth swim; to pass through your own plumbing, meet the worms within. And realize it. That you were. Under all the world. When I was a kid I lied like a sewer system. I told my sometime chums I went there. To the realm of shades. And said I saw vast halls, the many chambers of endless caves, magic pools guarded by Merlins dressed in mole fur and cobweb, chests overflowing with doubtless dime-store jewelry, rooms of doubloon, and, suddenly, through an opening jagged as a rip in rotten cloth, a new sun shining, meadows filled with healthy flowers, crayon-colored streams, oh, the acres of Edens inside ourselves . . .

"Meanwhile carry on without complaining. No arm with arm-band raised on high. No more booming bands, no searchlit skies. Or shall I, like the rivers, rise? Ah. Well. Is rising wise? Revolver like the Fuhrer near an ear. Or lay my mind down by sorrow's side."

This is no predictable apocalyptic reflex, surfacing out of the century's mist like a Loch Ness hallucination. This is a mourning, a requiem, a folding away of time's own future.

What becomes most compelling therefore, are the places and voices where the journey into the cellar of time does not end with a resounding slam of a door, but where the journey is a rescue of sorts, an excavation for the purposes of building, discovering, envisioning a future. I am not, of course, encouraging and anointing happy endings—forced or truly felt—or anointing bleak ones intended as correctives or warnings. I mean to call attention to whether the hand which holds the book's metaphors is an open palm or a fist.

In *The Salteaters,* Toni Cade Bambara opens this brilliant novel with a startling question: "Are you sure you want to be well?" Are you *sure* you want to be well? What flows from that very serious inquiry is a healing that requires a frightened modern day Demeter to fathom and sound every minute of her and her community's depths, to re-think and re-live the past—simply to answer that question. The success of her excavation is described in these terms:

". . . what had driven Velma into the oven . . . was nothing compared to what awaited her, was to come. . . . Of course she would fight it, Velma was a fighter. Of course she would reject what could not be explained in terms of words, notes, numbers or those other systems whose roots had been driven far underground. . . . Velma's next trial might lead to an act far more devastating than striking out at the body or swallowing gas.

"The patient turning smoothly on the stool, head thrown back about to shout, to laugh, to sing. No need of Minnie's hands now. That is clear. Velma's glow aglow and two yards wide of clear unstreaked white and yellow. Her eyes scanning the air surrounding Minnie, then examining her own hands, fingers stretched and radiant. No need of Minnie's hands now so the healer withdraws them, drops them in her lap just as Velma, rising on steady legs, throws off the shawl that drops down on the stool a burst cocoon."

The title of Salman Rushdie's latest novel, *The Moor's Last Sigh,* suggests the narrative will end on a death bed or in a graveyard. In fact it does. The storyteller/protagonist, Moreas Zogoiby, leads us on an exhilarating journey in order to nail his papers on the wall. Papers that are the result of his "daily, silent, singing for [his] daily life." Telling, writing, recording four generations of family and national history. A history of devastating loves, transcendent hatreds; of ambition without limit and sloth without redemption; loyalties beyond understanding and deceptions beyond imagination. When every step, every pause of this imaginary is finally surrendered to our view, this is the close:

"The rough grass in the graveyard has grown high and spikey and as I sit upon this tombstone I seem to be resting upon the grass's yellow points, weightless, floating free of burdens, borne aloft by a thick brush of miraculously unbending blades. I do not have long. My breaths are numbered, like the years of the ancient world, in reverse, and the countdown to zero is well advanced. I have used the last of my strength to make this pilgrimage. . . .

"At the head of this tombstone are three eroded letters; my fingertip reads them for me. RIP. Very well: I will rest, and hope for peace. The world is full of sleepers waiting for their moment of return . . . somewhere in a tangle of thorns, a beauty in a glass coffin awaits a prince's kiss. See: here is my flask. I'll drink some wine; and then, like a latter-day Van Winkle, I'll lay me down upon this graven stone, lay my head beneath these letters RIP, and close my eyes, according to our family's old practice of falling asleep in times of trouble, and hope to awaken, renewed and joyful, into a better time."

The rest, the peace is twice enunciated; but so is the hope. For renewal, joy and, most importantly, "a better time."

In 1990 Ben Okri ended his novel *The Famished Road,* with a dream so deeply felt it is prioritized over the entire narrative:

"The air in the room was calm. There were no turbulences. His [father's] presence protected our nightspace. There were no forms invading our air, pressing down on our roof, walking through the objects. The air was clear and wide. In my sleep I found open spaces where I floated without fear. The sweetness dissolved my tears. I was not afraid of Time.

"And then it was another morning . . .

"A dream can be the highest point in life."

In 1993, continuing the story of this sighted child, Okri concludes *Songs of Enchantment* with a more pronounced gesture toward the future:

"Maybe one day we will see the mountains ahead of us. Maybe one day we will see the seven mountains of our mysterious destiny. Maybe one day we will see that beyond our chaos there could always be a new sunlight, and serenity."

The symbolisms of the mountains he is referring to make up the opening of the book:

"We didn't see the seven mountains ahead of us. We didn't see how they are always ahead. Always calling us, always reminding us that there are more things to be done, dreams to be realized, joys to be re-discovered, promises made before birth to be fulfilled, beauty to be incarnated, and love embodied.

"We didn't notice how they hinted that nothing is ever finished, that struggles are never truly concluded, that sometimes we have to re-dream our lives, and that life can always be used to create more light."

The expectation in these lines is palpable, insistent on the possibility of "one great action lived out all the way to the sea, chang[ing] the history of the world."

Leslie Marmon Silko in *The Almanac of the Dead* flails and slashes through thousands of years of New World history, from centuries before the Conquistadors made their appearances on these shores to the current day. The novel rests on a timelessness that is not only past, but a future timelessness as well—time truly without end. The final image of this narrative is the snake spirit "pointing toward the South in the direction from which the people will come." The future tense of the verb is attached to a direction that is, unlike the directions of most comings we approve of, the south. And it is impossible to ignore the fact that it is precisely "the south" where walls, fences, armed guards and foaming hysteria are, at this very moment, gathering.

Cocoons from which healed women burst, dreams that take the terror from time, tombstone hopes for a better time, a time beyond chaos where the seven mountains of destiny lie, snake gods anticipating the people who will come from the south—these closing images following treks into the past lead one to hazard the conclusion that some writers disagree with prevailing notions of futurelessness. That they very much indeed not only have but insist on a future. That for them, for us, history is beginning again.

I am not ferreting out signs of tentative hope, obstinate optimism in contemporary fiction; I believe I am detecting an informed vision based on harrowing experience that nevertheless gestures toward a redemptive future. And I notice the milieu from which this vision rises. It is race inflected, gendered, colonialized, displaced, hunted.

There is an interesting trace here of divergent imaginaries, between the sadness of no more time, of the poignancy of inverted time—time that has only a past—of time itself living on "borrowed time," between that imaginary and the other one that has growing expectations of time with a relentless future. One looks to history for the feel of time or its purgative effects; one looks through history for its signs of renewal.

Literature, sensitive as a tuning fork, is an unblinking witness to the light and shade of the world we live in.

Beyond the world of literature, however, is another world; the world of commentary that has a quite other view of things. A Janus head that has masked its forward face and is at pains to assure us that the future is hardly worth the time. Perhaps it is the reality of a future as durable and far-reaching as the past, a future that will be shaped by those who have been pressed to the margins, by those who have been dismissed as irrelevant surplus, by those who have been cloaked with the demon's cape; perhaps it is the contemplation of that future that has occasioned the tremble of latter-day prophets afraid that the current disequalibrium is a stirring not an erasure. That not only is history not dead, but that it is about to take its first unfettered breath. Not soon, perhaps not in thirty years or fifty, because such a breath, such a massive intake, will take time. But it will be there. If that is so, then we should heed the meditations of literature. William Gass is correct. There are "acres of Edens inside ourselves." Time does have a future. Longer than its past and infinitely more hospitable—to the human race.

The Dancing Mind

Speech upon acceptance of the National Book Foundation Medal for Distinguished Contribution to American Letters. 6 November 1996. Reprinted by permission of International Creative Management, Inc. Copyright © 1996 by Toni Morrison.

There is a certain kind of peace that is not merely the absence of war. It is larger than that. The peace I am thinking of is not at the mercy of history's rule, nor is it a passive surrender to the status quo. The peace I am thinking of is the dance of an open mind when it engages another equally open one—an activity that occurs most naturally, most often in the reading/writing world we live in. Accessible as it is, this particular kind of peace warrants vigilance. The peril it faces comes not from the computers and information highways that raise alarm among book readers, but from unrecognized, more sinister quarters.

I want to tell two little stories—anecdotes really—that circle each other in my mind. They are disparate, unrelated anecdotes with more to distinguish each one from the other than similarities, but they are connected for me in a way that I hope to make clear.

The first I heard third- or fourth-hand, and although I can't vouch for its accuracy, I do have personal knowledge of situations exactly like it. A student at a very, very prestigious university said that it was in graduate school while working on his Ph.D. that he had to teach

188 POLITICS AND SOCIETY

himself a skill he had never learned. He had grown up in an affluent community with very concerned and caring parents. He said that his whole life had been filled with carefully selected activities: educational, cultural, athletic. Every waking hour was filled with events to enhance his life. Can you see him? Captain of his team. Member of the Theatre Club. A Latin Prize winner. Going on vacations designed for pleasure and meaningfulness; on fascinating and educational trips and tours; attending excellent camps along with equally highly motivated peers. He gets the best grades, is a permanent fixture on the honor roll, gets into several of the best universities, graduates, goes on to get a master's degree, and now is enrolled in a Ph.D. program at this first-rate university. And it is there that (at last, but fortunately) he discovers his disability: in all those years he had never learned to sit in a room by himself and read for four hours and have those four hours followed by another four without any companionship but his own mind. He said it was the hardest thing he ever had to do, but he taught himself, forced himself to be alone with a book he was not assigned to read, a book on which there was no test. He forced himself to be alone without the comfort of disturbance of telephone, radio, television. To his credit, he learned this habit, this skill, that once was part of any literate young person's life.

The second story involves a first-hand experience. I was in Strasbourg attending a meeting of a group called the Parliament of Writers. It is an organization of writers committed to the aggressive rescue of persecuted writers. After one of the symposia, just outside the doors of the hall, a woman approached me and asked if I knew anything about the contemporary literature of her country. I said no; I knew nothing of it. We talked a few minutes more. Earlier, while listening to her speak on a panel, I had been awestruck by her articulateness, the ease with which she moved among languages and literatures, her familiarity with histories of nations, histories of criticisms, histories of authors. She knew my work; I knew nothing of hers. We continued to talk, animatedly, and then, in the middle of it, she began to cry. No sobs, no heaving shoulders, just great tears rolling down her face. She did not wipe them away and she did not loosen her gaze. "You have to help us," she said. "You have to help us. They are shooting us down in the street." By "us" she meant women who wrote against the grain. "What can I do?" I asked her. She said, "I don't know, but you have to try. There isn't anybody else."

Both of those stories are comments on the contemporary reading/writing life. In one, a comfortable, young American, a "successfully" educated male, alien in his own company, stunned and hampered by the inadequacy of his fine education, resorts to autodidactic strategies to move outside the surfeit and bounty and excess and (I think) the terror of growing up vacuum-pressured in this country and to learn a very old-fashioned skill. In the other, a splendidly educated woman living in a suffocating regime writes in fear that death may very well be the consequence of doing what I do: as a woman to write and publish unpoliced narrative. The danger of both environments is striking. First, the danger to reading that our busied-up, education-as-horse-race, trophy-driven culture poses even to the entitled; second, the physical danger to writing suffered by persons with enviable educations who live in countries where the practice of modern art is illegal and subject to official vigilantism and murder.

I have always doubted and disliked the therapeutic claims made on behalf of writing and writers. Writing never made me happy. Writing never made me suffer. I have had misfortunes small and large, yet all through them nothing could keep me from doing it. And nothing could satiate my appetite for others who did. What is so important about this craft that it dominates me and my colleagues? A craft that appears solitary but needs another for its completion. A craft that signals independence but relies totally on an industry. It is more than an urge to make sense artfully or to believe it matters. It is more than a desire to watch other writers manage to refigure the world. I know now, more than I ever did (and I always on some level knew it), that I need that intimate, sustained surrender to the company of my own mind while it touches another's—which is reading: what the graduate student taught himself. That I need to offer the fruits of my own imaginative intelligence to another without fear of anything more deadly than disdain—which is writing: what the woman writer fought a whole government to do.

The reader disabled by an absence of solitude; the writer imperiled by the absence of a hospitable community. Both stories fuse and underscore for me the seriousness of the industry whose sole purpose is the publication of writers for readers. It is a business, of course, in which there is feasting, and even some coin; there is drama and high, high spirits. There is celebration and anguish, there are flukes and errors in judgment; there is brilliance and unbridled ego. But that is the costume. Underneath the cut of bright and dazzling cloth, pulsing beneath the jewelry, the life of the book world is quite serious. Its real life is about creating and producing and distributing knowledge; about making it possible for the entitled as well as the dispossessed to experience one's own mind dancing with another's; about making sure that the environment in which this work is done is welcoming, supportive. It is making sure that no encroachment of private wealth, government control, or cultural expediency can interfere with what gets written or published. That no conglomerate or political wing uses its force to still inquiry or to reaffirm rule.

Securing that kind of peace—the peace of the dancing mind—is our work, and, as the woman in Strasbourg said, "There isn't anybody else."

How Can Values Be Taught in the University

Paper delivered at the Center for Human Values, Princeton University, 27 April 2000. Printed in the *Michigan Quarterly Review* 40.2 (2001): 273–78. Reprinted by permission of International Creative Management, Inc. Copyright © 2000 by Toni Morrison.

It is the right question and I think appropriately the first one, glancing away, as it does, from an associated, perhaps even precursor one: *whether* universities should teach values. The "whether" ripples through late twentieth-century debates in several forms. Certain disciplines pride themselves on the value-free nature of their intellectual inquiries, and the pursuit of "objectivity" is at the heart of their claims, claims which are understood to place the stature of these disciplines far above interpretive ones.

Nevertheless, explicitly or implicitly, the university has always taught (by which I mean examined, evaluated, posited, reinforced) values, and I should think will always follow or circle the track of its origins. When higher education leapt or strutted out of the doors of the church (whether by license from the crown, permission of the diocese, or charters from guilds), it was extricating itself from the church's charge, where monastic schools and libraries were centers of learning and most students were expected to take (and did take) orders—ecclesiastical orders, that is—but it did not slam the cathedral doors or the Calvinist parish gates behind itself. The faculty-cum-clergy carried their religious principles and preoccupations with them. Like other institutions of higher learning, Princeton was founded by a collection of laymen and clergy who, because of a dispute concerning religious belief and the dissemination of those beliefs to its student body, exited a college founded by other clergy and laymen. The founding of the university was never understood to be a severance from ecclesiastical scholarship, but rather a segue into the more exciting and demanding realm of the conjunction of faith and reason—applying reason to faith, faith to the worldly, and abjuring the shadow of scholasticism which tainted both. The history of moral philosophy and its transformation into humanistic studies can be seen as an argument with and among definitions of reason, its status in spiritual life, and its impact not on faith, but on moral orientation.

The genesis of higher education is unabashedly theological and conscientiously value-ridden and value-seeking. There is not much point in and certainly not much time for rehearsing the evolution of the university to its present state of arrest over questions of value and ethics. We can simply note that the academy has, for the most part, shed its theological coat, relegated those high purposes to departments, schools of religion, and seminaries, and wrapped itself instead in a moral cape made of panels of cloth woven in enlightened and pre-enlightenment theses: that knowledge is a good; that the rightly trained mind would turn toward virtue; that the commitment of higher education was to train leaders to envision, if not effect, a desirable future.

The university's re-invention of itself and its mission responded to major historical upheavals: wars, transformations in economy,

new populations, etc., and as newer, better, and more likely prov-
able knowledge accumulated in the sciences, the shift in the goals
of universities was dramatic and may have led some to think that
the secular education offered by the academy strives only for value-
free, objective, pure research, analysis and exposition. Yet today,
biological and medical sciences are being perpetually transformed
by the ethical consequences of their own innovations. Education in
the law is similarly scoured by its own practitioners employing new
technologies to concepts of justice. All kinds of disciplines are responding to modern ethical issues with the same ferocity as their
predecessors, ancient, medieval, or colonial. Although no one would
suggest that corporate and commercial interests in the universities
are innocent and not vested, it is strongly asserted that those interests serve in some way "the public good." Thus the real or imagined
search for "goodness" in some figuration is still part of the justifying,
legitimizing language of the academy.

It is in that context that the question is put: how to teach values?
Several initiatives are already in place at many universities (certainly
at Princeton) which constitute a kind of secular pulpit: the encour-
agement of voluntarism, an announced high regard and reward for
students engaged in public service work; policy measures instituted
by administrators to protect and defend their populations from ha-
rassment and assaults on their liberty and safety; careful and medi-
ated responses to civil rights legislation; regular voluntary examinations of itself for inequities of representation; the creation of institutes
and centers funded for precisely the airing and pursuit of ethical
questions and allied problems of inculcating value (not least of which
is the sponsor of this conference—the University Center for Human
Values). These efforts (often bitterly contested) can impress upon

the student body the seriousness in which the university holds these matters—a seriousness which stresses and clarifies the university's definition of a complete and sophisticated education. But institutional directives can become formulaic, a menu of phrases, courses, and temporary forms of behavior that a student can taste without swallowing. Or, more cynically, they work as "fictions," folk costumes which the site of learning wears to cover the nakedness of mandarin, exclusionary domination.

Yet as assaults on and demands for school prayer, religious symbols on school property, and control of course curricula become legal cases making their way through courts, frequently invoking the separation of state and church, that legal journey both skirts and displays another question: not whether or how, but which. Which values, in act or symbol, should a public institution of learning reject, endorse, or tolerate? To insist that it endorse none, that it remain neutral, non-judgmental, and tolerant of religions, religiosity, and atheists alike, requires a sensitivity and alertness so intense it can descend to the absurd when not merely distracting. Why should schools close on religious holidays? Why should they be called *holi* as in holy days? Why permit houses of worship to participate in school and academic functions? I am merely suggesting how porous the "separation" of church and state is, how irrevocably entangled are our lives, our practices, and our language in passionately held views of what the good, the ethical, the moral mean or should mean; how passionate the clash of reason and faith; of genetics and environment. These are the Great Debates of the twenty-first century as the struggle to improve the world goes on. This is familiar ground upon which humanistic inquiry treads. Recent inquiries have considered whether our or any notion of secular morality is "universal." Whether whole bodies of knowledge are secret agendas of oppression. Whether "evil" is simply another aesthetic; whether violence has its own "beauty" in art, in cultural practice, in politics.

I have no original ideas in this matter or on this score. The torturous route the academy has taken to shake off scholasticism and embrace humanism is its own best evidence of the magnitude of the question. I tend to think, however, that in the course of teaching, the material I ask students to read, the dialogue that ensues following those readings, and the threads of argument I nudge students to explore, make up one part of how I communicate value. But it may not be the most important part. I know, as you do, from having been a student and from observing faculty as well as being a member of many faculties, that the values one personally holds seep through. Through everything I say, write, and do, however I may try to stand between, to the side, or over issues of ethics and value when discussion is underway, my position is either known or available to be known. If I encourage strictly and only aesthetic readings of literature, then I have left an indelible message of where I place the persuasive, historical aspects of literature. If I insist upon solely political understandings of these readings, that too is a teaching of value. If I am content with or indifferent to the purification rites of the justice and legal system in the way it handles its young, its minorities, that is a powerful value judgment not hidden although it may be unspoken. Is my critique fruitful or merely elaborate name-calling or put-down?

What I think and do is already inscribed on my teaching, my work. And so should it be. We teach values by having them. Whether or not we drive or seduce or persuade others to share them, whether or not we are indifferent to or accommodating to the ethics of others, whether we are amused by the concept of value being teachable, whether we are open to being argued into supporting values contrary to those we have held—all of these possibilities and strategies matter. The innate feature of the university is that not only does it examine, it also produces power-laden and value-ridden discourse. Much scholarship is often, even habitually, entangled in or regulated by ideology. Since, as humanists we know that that is the case, acknowledgment is preferable to the mask of disinterest. In any case, it becomes incumbent upon us as citizen/scholars in the university to accept the consequences of our own value-redolent roles. Like it or not, we are paradigms of our own values, advertisements of our own ethics—especially noticeable when we presume to foster ethics-free, value-lite education. Now the question of how to teach values becomes less fraught. How do we treat each other? The members of our own profession? How do we respond to professional and political cunning, to raw and ruthless ambition, to the plight of those outside our walls? What are we personally willing to sacrifice, give up for the "public good"? What gestures of reparation are we personally willing to make? What risky, unfashionable research are we willing to undertake?

The evolution (or devolution, depending upon one's point of view) of the university into an internet of higher education, with texts and their explications data-based, with interrogations routinized, with experts taking the place of professors, is not to be confined to fantasy. Ideas for just such expansion are already in practice, and its worth to third world, rural, and under-served communities is hard to gainsay. But a massive conversion to a www.com university may not be our complete or immediate future only because the human desire to congregate is paramount. But another reason for the survival of more traditional campuses (with living, fleshed, as opposed to virtual persons interacting with students, contributing to something called "student life" and the benefits thereof) is that survival may depend on the move from the *profession* of humanistic intellectual to the *vocation* of humanistic intellectual, regardless of the dangers of demagoguery. If the critical platform remains open, the charlatans will be exposed.

Post-Reagan business centers have turned much academic and public discourse back to nineteenth-century liberalism. To counter the deleterious effects of that combination of nostalgia and hypocrisy, the university need not return to its pre-medieval, medieval, or colonial sources to re-ignite wider and more variable notions of virtue, civitas, response-ability and freedom. It can speculate instead on a future where the poor are not yet, not quite, all dead; where the under-represented minorities are not quite all imprisoned. In that recipe for American pie in which a society made up of an increasingly toughened crust of the rich continues to rest upon and contain the seething, smarting poor, then strategizing and updating the means by which values are taught becomes critical. If the university does not take seriously and rigorously its role as guardian of wider civic freedoms, as interrogator of more and more complex ethical problems, as servant and preserver of deeper democratic practices, then some other regime or ménage of regimes will do it for us, in spite of us, and without us.

The Nobel Lecture in Literature

Stockholm, 7 December 1993. From *Nobel Lectures, Literature 1991–1995*, edited by Sture Allén. Singapore: World Scientific Publishing Co., 1997. Reprinted by permission of International Creative Management, Inc. Copyright © 1993 by Toni Morrison.

"Once upon a time there was an old woman. Blind but wise." Or was it an old man? A guru, perhaps. Or a griot soothing restless children. I have heard this story, or one exactly like it, in the lore of several cultures.

"Once upon a time there was an old woman. Blind. Wise."

In the version I know the woman is the daughter of slaves, black, American, and lives alone in a small house outside of town. Her reputation for wisdom is without peer and without question. Among her people she is both the law and its transgression. The honor she is paid and the awe in which she is held reach beyond her neighborhood to places far away; to the city where the intelligence of rural prophets is the source of much amusement.

One day the woman is visited by some young people who seem to be bent on disproving her clairvoyance and showing her up for the fraud they believe she is. Their plan is simple: they enter her house and ask the one question the answer to which rides solely on her difference from them, a difference they regard as a profound disability: her blindness. They stand before her, and one of them says,

"Old woman, I hold in my hand a bird. Tell me whether it is living or dead."

She does not answer, and the question is repeated. "Is the bird I am holding living or dead?"

Still she doesn't answer. She is blind and cannot see her visitors, let alone what is in their hands. She does not know their color, gender or homeland. She only knows their motive.

The old woman's silence is so long, the young people have trouble holding their laughter.

Finally she speaks and her voice is soft but stern. "I don't know," she says. "I don't know whether the bird you are holding is dead or alive, but what I do know is that it is in your hands. It is in your hands."

Her answer can be taken to mean: if it is dead, you have either found it that way or you have killed it. If it is alive, you can still kill it. Whether it is to stay alive, it is your decision. Whatever the case, it is your responsibility.

For parading their power and her helplessness, the young visitors are reprimanded, told they are responsible not only for the act of mockery but also for the small bundle of life sacrificed to achieve its aims. The blind woman shifts attention away from assertions of power to the instrument through which that power is exercised.

Speculation on what (other than its own frail body) that bird-in-the-hand might signify has always been attractive to me, but especially so now thinking, as I have been, about the work I do that has brought me to this company. So I choose to read the bird as language and the woman as a practiced writer. She is worried about how the language she dreams in, given to her at birth, is handled, put into service, even withheld from her for certain nefarious purposes. Being a writer she thinks of language partly as a system, partly as a living thing over which one has control, but mostly as agency—as an act with consequences. So the question the children put to her—"Is it living or dead?"—is not unreal because she thinks of language as susceptible to death, erasure; certainly imperiled and salvageable only by an effort of the will. She believes that if the bird in the hands of her visitors is dead the custodians are responsible for the corpse. For her a dead language is not only one no longer spoken or written, it is unyielding language content to admire its own paralysis. Like statist language, censored and censoring. Ruthless in its policing duties, it has no desire or purpose other than maintaining the free range of its own narcotic narcissism, its own exclusivity and dominance. However moribund, it is not without effect for it actively thwarts the intellect, stalls conscience, suppresses human potential. Unreceptive to interrogation, it cannot form or tolerate new ideas, shape other thoughts, tell another story, fill baffling silences. Official language smitheryed to sanction ignorance and preserve privilege is a suit of armor polished to shocking glitter, a husk from which the knight departed long ago. Yet there it is: dumb, predatory, sentimental. Exciting reverence in schoolchildren, providing shelter for despots, summoning false memories of stability, harmony among the public.

She is convinced that when language dies, out of carelessness, disuse, indifference and absence of esteem, or killed by fiat, not only she herself, but all users and makers are accountable for its demise. In her country children have bitten their tongues off and use bullets instead to iterate the voice of speechlessness, of disabled and disabling language, of language adults have abandoned altogether as a device for grappling with meaning, providing guidance, or expressing love. But she knows tongue-suicide is not only the choice of children. It is common among the infantile heads of state and power merchants whose evacuated language leaves them with no access to what is left of their human instincts for they speak only to those who obey, or in order to force obedience.

The systematic looting of language can be recognized by the tendency of its users to forgo its nuanced, complex, mid-wifery properties for menace and subjugation. Oppressive language does more than represent violence; it is violence; does more than represent the limits of knowledge; it limits knowledge. Whether it is obscuring state language or the faux-language of mindless media; whether it is the proud but calcified language of the academy or the commodity driven language of science; whether it is the malign language of law-without-ethics, or language designed for the estrangement of minorities, hiding its racist plunder in its literary cheek—it must be rejected, altered and exposed. It is the language that drinks blood, laps vulnerabilities, tucks its fascist boots under crinolines of respectability and patriotism as it moves relentlessly toward the bottom line and the bottomed-out mind. Sexist language, racist language, theistic language—all are typical of the policing languages of mastery, and cannot, do not permit new knowledge or encourage the mutual exchange of ideas.

The old woman is keenly aware that no intellectual mercenary, nor insatiable dictator, no paid-for politician or demagogue; no counterfeit journalist would be persuaded by her thoughts. There is and will be rousing language to keep citizens armed and arming; slaughtered and slaughtering in the malls, courthouses, post offices, playgrounds, bedrooms and boulevards; stirring, memorializing language to mask the pity and waste of needless death. There will be more diplomatic language to countenance rape, torture, assassination. There is and will be more seductive, mutant language designed to throttle women, to pack their throats like paté-producing geese with their own unsayable, transgressive words; there will be more of the language of surveillance disguised as research; of politics and history calculated to render the suffering of millions mute; language glamorized to thrill the dissatisfied and bereft into assaulting their neighbors; arrogant pseudo-empirical language crafted to lock creative people into cages of inferiority and hopelessness.

Underneath the eloquence, the glamor, the scholarly associations, however stirring or seductive, the heart of such language is languishing, or perhaps not beating at all—if the bird is already dead.

She has thought about what could have been the intellectual history of any discipline if it had not insisted upon, or been forced into, the waste of time and life that rationalizations for and representations of dominance required—lethal discourses of exclusion blocking access to cognition for both the excluder and the excluded.

The conventional wisdom of the Tower of Babel story is that the collapse was a misfortune. That it was the distraction, or the weight of many languages that precipitated the tower's failed architecture. That one monolithic language would have expedited the building and heaven would have been reached. Whose heaven, she wonders? And what kind? Perhaps the achievement of Paradise was premature, a little hasty if no one could take the time to understand other languages, other views, other narratives period. Had they, the heaven they imagined might have been found at their feet. Complicated, demanding, yes, but a view of heaven as life; not heaven as post-life.

She would not want to leave her young visitors with the impression that language should be forced to stay alive merely to be. The vitality of language lies in its ability to limn the actual, imagined and possible lives of its speakers, readers, writers. Although its poise is sometimes in displacing experience it is not a substitute for it. It arcs toward the place where meaning may lie. When a President of the United States thought about the graveyard his country had become, and said, "The world will little note nor long remember what we say here. But it will never forget what they did here," his simple words are exhilarating in their life-sustaining properties because they refused to encapsulate the reality of 600,000 dead men in a cataclysmic race war. Refusing to monumentalize, disdaining the "final word," the precise "summing up," acknowledging their "poor power to add or detract," his words signal deference to the uncapturability of the life it mourns. It is the deference that moves her, that recognition that language can never live up to life once and for all. Nor should it. Language can never "pin down" slavery, genocide, war. Nor should it yearn for the arrogance to be able to do so. Its force, its felicity is in its reach toward the ineffable.

Be it grand or slender, burrowing, blasting, or refusing to sanctify; whether it laughs out loud or is a cry without an alphabet, the choice word, the chosen silence, unmolested language surges toward knowledge, not its destruction. But who does not know of literature banned because it is interrogative; discredited because it is critical; erased because alternate? And how many are outraged by the thought of a self-ravaged tongue?

Word-work is sublime, she thinks, because it is generative; it makes meaning that secures our difference, our human difference—the way in which we are like no other life.

We die. That may be the meaning of life. But we do language. That may be the measure of our lives.

"Once upon a time, . . . " visitors ask an old woman a question. Who are they, these children? What did they make of that encounter? What did they hear in those final words: "The bird is in your hands"? A sentence that gestures towards possibility or one that drops a latch? Perhaps what the children heard was "It's not my problem. I am old, female, black, blind. What wisdom I have now is in knowing I cannot help you. The future of language is yours."

They stand there. Suppose nothing was in their hands? Suppose the visit was only a ruse, a trick to get to be spoken to, taken seriously as they have not been before? A chance to interrupt, to violate the adult world, its miasma of discourse about them, for them, but never to them? Urgent questions are at stake, including the one they have asked: "Is the bird we hold living or dead?" Perhaps the question meant: "Could someone tell us what is life? What is death?" No trick at all; no silliness. A straightforward question worthy of the attention of a wise one. An old one. And if the old and wise who have lived life and faced death cannot describe either, who can?

But she does not; she keeps her secret; her good opinion of herself; her gnomic pronouncements; her art without commitment. She keeps her distance, enforces it and retreats into the singularity of isolation, in sophisticated, privileged space.

Nothing, no word follows her declaration of transfer. That silence is deep, deeper than the meaning available in the words she has spoken. It shivers, this silence, and the children, annoyed, fill it with language invented on the spot.

"Is there no speech," they ask her, "no words you can give us that helps us break through your dossier of failures? Through the education you have just given us that is no education at all because we are paying close attention to what you have done as well as to what you have said? To the barrier you have erected between generosity and wisdom?

"We have no bird in our hands, living or dead. We have only you and our important question. Is the nothing in our hands something you could not bear to contemplate, to even guess? Don't you remember being young when language was magic without meaning? When what you could say, could not mean? When the invisible was what imagination strove to see? When questions and demands for answers burned so brightly you trembled with fury at not knowing?

"Do we have to begin consciousness with a battle heroines and heroes like you have already fought and lost leaving us with nothing in our hands except what you have imagined is there? Your answer is artful, but its artfulness embarrasses us and ought to embarrass you. Your answer is indecent in its self-congratulation. A made-for-television script that makes no sense if there is nothing in our hands.

"Why didn't you reach out, touch us with your soft fingers, delay the sound bite, the lesson, until you knew who we were? Did you so despise our trick, our modus operandi you could not see that we were baffled about how to get your attention? We are young. Unripe. We have heard all our short lives that we have to be responsible. What could that possibly mean in the catastrophe this world has become; where, as a poet said, "nothing needs to be exposed since it is already barefaced." Our inheritance is an affront. You want us to have your old, blank eyes and see only cruelty and mediocrity. Do you think we are stupid enough to perjure ourselves again and again with the fiction of nationhood? How dare you talk to us of duty when we stand waist deep in the toxin of your past?

"You trivialize us and trivialize the bird that is not in our hands. Is there no context for our lives? No song, no literature, no poem full of vitamins, no history connected to experience that you can pass along to help us start strong? You are an adult. The old one, the wise one. Stop thinking about saving your face. Think of our lives and tell us your particularized world. Make up a story. Narrative is radical, creating us at the very moment it is being created. We will not blame you if your reach exceeds your grasp; if love so ignites your words they go down in flames and nothing is left but their scald. Or if, with the reticence of a surgeon's hands, your words suture only the places where blood might flow. We know you can never do it properly—once and for all. Passion is never enough; neither is skill. But try. For our sake and yours forget your name in the street; tell us what the world has been to you in the dark places and in the light. Don't tell us what to believe, what to fear. Show us belief's wide skirt and the stitch that unravels fear's caul. You, old woman, blessed with blindness, can speak the language that tells us what only language can: how to see without pictures. Language alone protects us from the scariness of things with no names. Language alone is meditation.

"Tell us what it is to be a woman so that we may know what it is to be a man. What moves at the margin. What it is to have no home in this place. To be set adrift from the one you knew. What it is to live at the edge of towns that cannot bear your company.

"Tell us about ships turned away from shorelines at Easter, placenta in a field. Tell us about a wagonload of slaves, how they sang so softly their breath was indistinguishable from the falling snow. How they knew from the hunch of the nearest shoulder that the next stop would be their last. How, with hands prayered in their sex, they thought of heat, then sun. Lifting their faces as though it was there for the taking. Turning as though there for the taking. They stop at an inn. The driver and his mate go in with the lamp leaving them humming in the dark. The horse's void steams into the snow beneath its hooves and its hiss and melt are the envy of the freezing slaves.

"The inn door opens: a girl and a boy step away from its light. They climb into the wagon bed. The boy will have a gun in three years, but now he carries a lamp and a jug of warm cider. They pass it from mouth to mouth. The girl offers bread, pieces of meat and something more: a glance into the eyes of the one she serves. One helping for each man, two for each woman. And a look. They look back. The next stop will be their last. But not this one. This one is warmed."

It's quiet again when the children finish speaking, until the woman breaks into the silence.

Finally, she says, "I trust you now. I trust you with the bird that is not in your hands because you have truly caught it. Look. How lovely it is, this thing we have done—together."

Index